Better Homes and Gardens®

garden decorating

Better Homes and Gardens® Books
Des Moines, Iowa

Better Homes and Gardens® Books
An imprint of Meredith® Books

Garden Decorating
Writer: Julie A. Martens
Editor and Project Manager: Kate Carter Frederick
Art Director: Lyne Neymeyer
Project Coordinator: Beth Ann Edwards
Photo Coordinator: Lois Sutherland
Copy Chief: Terri Fredrickson
Copy and Production Editor: Victoria Forlini
Editorial Operations Manager: Karen Schirm
Managers, Book Production: Pam Kvitne, Marjorie J. Schenkelberg
Contributing Copy Editor: Sharon McHaney
Contributing Proofreaders: Fran Gardner, Terri Krueger, Kathy Roth Eastman
Contributing Technical Editor: David Haupert
Technical Consultant: Amy Pruitt
Illustrator: Tom Rosborough
Indexer: Deborah L. Baier
Inputter: Connie Webb
Electronic Production Coordinator: Paula Forest
Editorial and Design Assistants: Mary Lee Gavin, Karen McFadden, Kathy Stevens

Meredith® Books
Publisher and Editor in Chief: James D. Blume
Design Director: Matt Strelecki
Managing Editor: Gregory H. Kayko
Executive Editor, Home Improvement and Gardening: Benjamin W. Allen
Executive Editor, Gardening: Michael McKinley

Director, Production: Douglas M. Johnston

Vice President and General Manager: Douglas J. Guendel

Better Homes and Gardens® Magazine
Editor in Chief: Karol DeWulf Nickell
Deputy Editor, Gardens and Outdoor Living: Mark Kane

Meredith Publishing Group
President, Publishing Group: Stephen M. Lacy
Vice President-Publishing Director: Bob Mate

Meredith Corporation
Chairman and Chief Executive Officer: William T. Kerr

Chairman of the Executive Committee: E. T. Meredith III

All of us at Better Homes and Gardens® Books are dedicated to providing you with information and ideas to enhance your home and garden. We welcome your comments and suggestions. Write to us at: Better Homes and Gardens Books, Garden Editorial Department, 1716 Locust St., Des Moines, IA 50309-3023.

If you would like to purchase any of our gardening, cooking, crafts, home improvement, or home decorating and design books, check wherever quality books are sold. Or visit us at bhgbooks.com

Cover photograph: Ed Gohlich

garden decorating

introduction

garden decor

A beautifully planted garden draws interest and inspires wonder. But a beautifully decorated garden includes other elements that blend with the plants to make a setting that's attractive and complete. The place exudes a sense of design, as well as comfort and personality.

What's more, a well-decorated garden makes your outdoor spaces more useful and rewarding. By planning carefully and including certain elements, you minimize maintenance chores and maximize privacy. Even the smallest spaces benefit from embellishments, from a sparkling fountain or birdbath to a musical wind chime or comfy chair.

Begin your decorating adventure here. On the following pages, you'll gather plenty of ideas and inspiration to help you through the process.

simple touches
below: **Everyday objects, such as pots and a bench, combine in a setting that epitomizes effective garden decoration.**

Use the tips and projects to make as many additions to your garden as your dreams allow.

First, contemplate your garden's style. Using this unifying principle creates cohesiveness between house and garden, plus it provides an outlet for personal expression. Explore the design approaches on the pages ahead and see which ones mesh with your style. At this point, look at the big picture and start to consider which decorating materials seem most appropriate for your garden.

structures unify
above: Use architectural elements, such as window-framing lattices, to unite house and garden. Upright structures also provide more growing room for plants.

favorite things
left: Add a comfortable chair, a sturdy table, and a quirky accent to a quiet corner, and voilà! What better place to sit and savor homegrown tomatoes, read, or listen to the birds sing?

introduction

good garden bones

Whether you're breaking ground on a new garden or you're an old hand with a hoe, your garden can benefit from structural embellishments.

To establish the framework of a garden, start with floor and wall treatments. Choose surfaces for underfoot, such as grassy paths, gravel, or stepping-stones. If you already have a deck or patio, consider dressing it up with a painted area rug. Spiff up walls with trellises, either cloaked with vines or left bare to show their structural form.

Think about the entrances to your garden and outdoor living areas. Would an arbor or a gate help direct traffic and make the area more welcoming or private? Adding an arbor gives you an opportunity to grow the climbing fragrant rose you've always wanted.

living wallpaper

right: **Spruce up walls with trellises and vines. Rely on simplicity by choosing a classic garden design icon, such as a picket fence.**

finishing touches

right: **Decorate an entry with charming statuary or potted plants set atop pillars. The gate welcomes visitors.**

bird's-eye view

far right: **Use a birdbath as a cool oasis for a potted plant (set the pot on rocks to avoid immersing it in the water).**

decor resources

Highlight the natural attributes of your garden as you devise your decorating plans. In wide open spaces, wind art comes to life as breezes drift through. Mask neighborhood noise with a trickling fountain formed from cast-off garden hoses or with a tinkling wind chime made from dangling silverware. Transform a shady nook into a luxuriously cozy corner by adding cushioned chairs and candles. Do all this and more on a limited budget by working with things you already have.

classy corner

left: Decorative elements abound in this corner garden next to the house. A wall trellis, a window box, and a small pond with a waterfall combine with plants to make a pleasing setting.

introduction

garden artistry

To decorate your garden, combine beauty and practicality. When adding decor to your garden, ask yourself two questions. First, ask: "Is it me?" Select accessories that reflect your personal style and tastes. Add elements that you adore, not just those that you think will look good or happen to be on sale. A ho-hum garden overflows with unrelated items. An inviting garden emanates personality when it features a theme that's taken years to create, a one-of-a-kind sculpture acquired on a memorable trip, or a favorite color that's repeated throughout.

Second, ask: "Do the decorative elements serve other purposes?" Dressing up the functional aspects of a garden, from paths and edges to plant supports and containers, boosts a garden's effectiveness visually, as well as practically.

plan for change

Aim for artful simplicity. The larger the piece, whether art or furnishing, the more impact you'll achieve. Adding lots of small pieces may result in clutter.

Remember that outdoor decor fades, weathers, and deteriorates over time. Change is inevitable in the garden, in the accessories as well as in the plantings. Honor that natural process by incorporating art that's versatile, changeable, and movable. But first make sure your furnishings are the most well-made and long-lasting ones that your budget allows.

fancy flight

right: **Turn ordinary steps into a potted garden with a collection of unusual containers and a few decorative elements. An earthy theme of terra-cotta and gray spherical shapes dominates this scene. Pots and pedestals create additional layers of interest.**

Whether you're planning a new garden or scrutinizing an existing one, think about safety and convenience. For instance, can you stroll your garden paths without stumbling, even in the dark? Does your outdoor furniture store easily and require little upkeep? Could cushions make your garden more comfortable?

Perhaps it's time to update your garden by trading the railroad ties that frame planting areas with interlocking stone; or swap that old Jacuzzi for a low-maintenance fountain.

do yourself proud

Trade your trowel for a hammer or paintbrush and see what kind of garden decor comes to life beneath your hands. Throughout this book, you'll discover project after project for your garden, including wonderfully doable ideas, from fences and stepping-stones to seating and plant supports.

Each project features a complete materials list, as well as a quick-glance summary of the time and skill required. Also included is a cost guide, indicated by dollar signs. A "$" indicates that the project can be built for $50 or less. Projects costing $51–$100 are "$$"; projects costing more than $100 are indicated with "$$$."

Follow our plans step-by-step or use them as a springboard for your own creations. Making some of the items to decorate your garden will enhance your sense of pride and satisfaction.

Whether you're planting bulbs or building an elegant garden path, you'll find expert gardening advice at **www.bhg.com/bkgarden**

cast in concrete
above: Take advantage of concrete's versatility by using it to anchor your garden's artful ambience. In this scene, handcast concrete art adds weatherproof form and sturdy substance with leaf sculpture and classic columns.

candle chandelier
left: Hang heavy items, such as a wrought-iron chandelier, from hardware designed to bear the weight. Keep candle flames well away from overhanging branches and other combustibles.

style

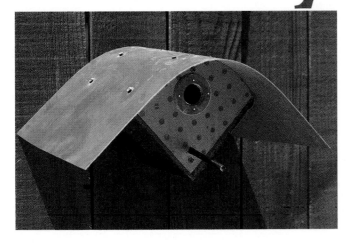

create a decor theme

A galvanized watering can easily becomes a classic element of garden style. Grouped in a character-rich collection, jazzed with a coat of bright paint, or overflowing with flowers, this everyday tool helps create a decorative theme. It shows your creative zeal and makes a personal statement.

style abounds As you survey the various garden styles on the following pages, pay attention to your reactions. Which gardens appeal the most to you and stir your enthusiasm and sense of comfort? Which styles would enhance your home and the existing elements of your landscape? Which design approaches reflect your personality and lifestyle?

Focus on style when you decorate your garden and it's more likely you'll be satisfied with the resulting cohesive, comfortable scene. Gather ideas and inspiration from the gardens shown and think about each style's hallmarks, from classical symmetry to tropical lushness, from artistically colorful to naturally rustic. Each style weaves a scene that starts with a few thematic anchors, including your choice of structures and furnishings.

gathering materials Once you determine your garden's style, choose appropriate materials and set the framework in place. Use floors and walls to define outdoor living spaces, whether creating new areas or updating existing ones.

Choose materials that fit your budget and your tastes, as well as functional needs for paths, edges, furnishings, and such. Let maintenance requirements influence your selection of surfaces throughout the garden. For instance, concrete proves long-lasting and easy to dress up. Give it artful appeal via crafty aging techniques. Locally quarried stone combines regional flair with easy care.

Some materials lend themselves to particular styles. Rock and bamboo represent cornerstones of Asian style; timber and twigs embody a rustic look. Imagine the possibilities of marrying sleek metallic lines with recycled glass blocks and carefree ornamental grasses in a contemporary setting. Combine decorative elements and blend styles to create your own, eclectic design.

classic

timeless looks

Classic garden design never goes out of style. Ordered and refined, the look is typically formal. Sharp, uncluttered lines help define garden spaces. Architectural elements play a major role in defining the classic style, from elaborate gazebos and stately columns to simple but elegant urns. Gardeners position focal points, such as statues, structures, and pots, purposefully throughout the classic garden to draw eyes and wandering feet.

gorgeous gazebo
right: **A stately garden house fits a small garden with ease. The open latticework allows surrounding plantings to show through. Flanking the entrance, a pair of tuteurs (pyramid trellises), represent a time-honored element in garden design.**

grand entrance

left: Separate garden rooms with simple and stylish paths. Classical urns perched atop pedestals add eye-catching height to a garden. Planters reflect the seasons, playing garden-room sentries when filled with pansies in spring, ferns or impatiens in summer, ornamental cabbage in fall, and decorative greens and berried twigs in winter. Incorporate a gate or arch as an entryway to your garden.

aged to perfection

Architectural elements, such as ornate containers, trellises, pergolas, and statuary, add character to a classic garden. Over time, they develop a rich patina that makes them look as if they have been rooted in the earth for generations. Transform gleaming new treasures for your garden into weathered beauties with these easy tricks:

- For concrete pots, wipe off the new and rub on the old by coating surfaces with black wax (ordinarily used on antiques).
- A mossy veneer is the understatement of established, ageless beauty. To seed moss onto concrete, terra-cotta, or brick, swirl a small handful of moss in a blender with buttermilk. Brush the buttermilk on surfaces to be mossed; then keep them shaded and moist. Moss will grow in seven to 10 days. On brick walkways, water regularly to keep moss healthy.
- If you're adding a wooden structure, wipe freshly painted, still wet surfaces with a damp rag to create an instant weathered finish. Experiment to create the look you want.
- In outdoor seating areas, cover pillows with vintage fabrics that match your garden's well-seasoned ambience.

classic

design basics

A garden that revolves around classic design unfolds with the precision of a symphony. Whether in one area or between rooms, focal points draw the eye through the garden, from strategically placed structures to statuary or containers. A seamless blend of beautifully tailored lines clothed in lush plantings with few color changes epitomizes this traditional style.

The functional parts of a classic garden include pathways, structures, benches, and containers. Choose materials for these elements on the basis of their durability, versatility, and architectural capacity. Concrete offers all these qualities. When laying paths and purchasing containers, choose concrete for all-weather wear year after year. It stands up to the elements with ease. Allow concrete or cast-iron containers to sit outside through the toughest winter weather and replant them in spring. However, move terra-cotta pots, which are vulnerable to frost damage, indoors or into a protected shelter in regions where temperatures dip below freezing.

Metal trellises, furniture, and other pieces also stand up to harsh winters. Select weather-resistant wood furniture made from teak or shorea for lasting enjoyment. If wood structures remain in place through cold, wet weather, check them each spring for weak spots or wear, and make necessary repairs.

posy-lined path

right: **A strong framework provides one key to a classic look. This concrete path provides an avenue or allée leading to spacious stepping-stones nestled in pea gravel. Striking structures pair handsomely with plantings. Subtle blooms and minimal color give the garden a cool, restful feel.**

On the softer side, use plantings as focal points. Tuck formal pedestal planters into a tangle of greenery. Manicure shrubs into neat shapes. In a tiny garden, place a graceful rose or a butterfly bush beneath a metal arch, creating a blooming focal point at the back of a planting bed or patio. In a larger garden, anchor a border planting with a weeping cypress or a tidy spruce, drawing the eye and suggesting the sense of permanence that a classic garden offers.

living room luxury

left: **The refined lines of an iron table, bench, and chairs transform a patio into an elegant retreat. A brick surface looks venerable and established with moss filling in the cracks. Frequent watering keeps the green carpet lush.**

parterre garden

left: **Symmetry represents a cornerstone of the classic look, rendered beautifully in a parterre design. This specialty garden features plants arranged in geometric patterns to create a sense of order. Boxwood suits a parterre, but if it is marginally hardy in your area, choose 'Northern Beauty' Japanese holly or dwarf balsam fir instead.**

artistic

blank canvas

For some gardeners, space unclaimed by hoe and trowel beckons like a blank canvas. An empty yard offers a clean start, begging for a composition of color and texture in eye-catching art. Brightly tinted furniture, containers, sculptural accents, and other captivating items splash bold colors throughout an artistic garden.

Let nature create pieces for your garden gallery. Let a tree stump provide sculptural beauty or have a boulder suggest monumental style. Whatever your artistic bent or preferred taste, use it to transform your garden into a work of art.

yen for beauty
right: **An oversize terra-cotta urn, lavender-painted planting boxes, and a series of metal arches provide simple yet captivating artistic flair in this garden canvas.**

When planning an artistic retreat, focus on color beyond blooms. Splash sunny paints on benches and sheds. Use unusual metallic finishes on furniture and pedestals.

Avoid getting carried away with an overabundance of art. One purposefully placed sculpture, whether fanciful or intense, transforms a corner of the garden into a lovely nook that commands attention. Set out an oversized pot to enthrall the eye with its voluptuous curves, for example. When placing your objets d'art, position seating nearby so you and others can enjoy the view.

helping hands
left: Unusual sculptural pieces easily find a home in the garden. These stone hands holding a concrete ball nestle among silvery *Artemisia* 'Powis Castle' and white *Zinnia angustifolia*. When you add art to an existing garden, set the piece in place for several days and move it around before you decide where to situate it permanently.

art for the ears
Art enthralls more than just the eye. There's a dimension of art that is heard as well.
- Breezes corralled by wind chimes play artful melodies that delight garden visitors. Choose chimes made from metal, shell, glass, or wood.
- Running water adds a soothing element to gardens. Capture the relaxing sound with a simple tabletop fountain, a bubbler pump in a container water garden, a dripper in a birdbath, or a full-scale water garden.

artistic

art in bloom

Tucking art into a living masterpiece of bud and bloom is easy. The basic rule: Use simple plantings in a simple color scheme.

Remember that the art should be a focal point. Choose plants that have foliage or flowers in tones complementary to (rather than competitive with) the artful element. Pair ferny foliage with blocky artistic elements. Plant soft-tone flowers in drifts of a single shade to skirt a colorful work of art.

When adding art to an existing bed, consider how plantings look through the seasons. A sculptural element that plays center stage in a spring perennial bed may be overgrown by midsummer.

Adequately anchor art objects destined as permanent parts of the garden. Move artwork into storage before cold weather arrives, if pieces need protection.

flying fish

above: Let your imagination—and your art—soar as you arrange your garden gallery. This metal fish-shape birdhouse perches high above a sea of *Tithonia* (Mexican sunflower). The pink shed accents this garden designer's artful approach.

towering fountain

left: Where space is limited, art does double duty. When possible, select art that blends function with fancy. This moss-topped pedestal serves as a fountain and as a focal point in the midst of container plantings. Water trickles down the pedestal to the pool below.

window dressing

below left: Simple plantings, like beautiful frames, help display garden art. Here, santolina topiaries perform perfectly in a plain metal window box. Metallic gold dry-brushed paint artfully tints and ties together the shutter cutouts and the window box.

rock around

below: Don't underestimate the artistic nature of rocks. A flagstone cistern cover, when adorned with a creative swirl of Japanese pebbles, becomes a garden centerpiece.

resourceful

old is new

Recycling proves stylish and savvy in a resourceful, vintage–oriented garden. Resourceful gardeners have vision. Their eyes see potential in what others call junk. No strangers to flea markets or roadside antique stands, resourceful gardeners hunt for treasures and finagle for bargains. They seek cast–off furniture, salvaged bricks, architectural moldings, and even the proverbial kitchen sink. If it can hold soil or water and plants, it's game for the garden. The joy of resourceful gardening is twofold: the thrill of the chase and the pleasure of working new treasures into the landscape.

all decked out

right: **This garden brims with salvaged accessories, but you could easily use fewer items to complete your garden's look. Invest in a few outstanding pieces to tuck among the plants.**

from castoff to container

Press pieces of the past into service as pots using these steps:

- Add drainage holes to containers. Invest in a masonry bit to drill through stone and metal surfaces.
- Instead of poking holes in priceless containers, use them as cachepots; slip a potted plant into a vintage container. Dump water that collects in the container.
- Line metal or wood containers with landscape fabric before adding soil to help stave off rust and rot.

outdoor carpeting

above: Dress up a wooden deck with a painted rug that exudes spontaneous informality. Begin with exterior enamel paint (leftover from another project, perhaps). Choose a color that complements your house. Add contrasting dots, swirls, circles, and curlicues when you daub on designs. For a unique carpet, incorporate a collage of family handprints (dip hands in paint; then press palm-down onto the surface). Paint pots to match the deck.

resourceful

lived-in look

Resourceful gardens host well-seasoned items that bring the past back to life. Unearthing treasures for your green space doesn't require a trip to exotic ports of call. The essence of vintage-oriented garden style comes from a blend of resourceful thriftiness. The best finds often happen close to home at rummage or estate sales, secondhand shops, or auctions.

A resourceful gardener's greatest challenge lies in tying it all together. A pile of junk remains a pile of junk in the garden unless it's tastefully incorporated with beautiful plantings. Give your collectibles a sense of cohesiveness by repeating design elements, such as materials, colors, and shapes throughout the garden.

salvaged seating

above: A vintage chair blends comfort with timeless style. When purchasing worn furniture, select sturdy pieces—unless you're buying them for planters or don't mind making repairs.

bed in bloom

right: A flower bed takes on new meaning when posies snuggle up to the frame of an antique iron bed turned trellis. Consider other uses for furniture. Dresser drawers form wonderful raised beds; an old bathtub becomes a water garden or keeps unruly plants (mint, running bamboo, or an ornamental grass) inbounds.

Start small with a piece of weathered furniture, a statue, or a planter for your first acquisition.

Plant in anything from washtubs to milk pails, but begin a collection of containers with one beautiful piece that you favor. Fill it with a single plant so the pot shines, and then group it with other character-rich containers.

tweet retreat
left: **This bird feeder boasts an ornate tin roof that was once a part of a ceiling. Don't worry if the item's finish is peeling, flaking, cracking, or rusting—it will fit the garden theme.**

rustic

back to nature

Constructing rustic, one-of-a-kind structures transforms castoffs of the natural world into artful, functional forms using scrap logs, branches, tree prunings, driftwood, and weedy tree saplings. Any gardener can master this art.

Acquiring the wood is easy. Seek local sources of native wood. Forage beaches or riverbanks for driftwood. Visit a construction site and ask the contractor if you can haul away cuttings. Scour curbs after heavy windstorms or traipse wooded areas for fallen branches. If asked, utility or tree service crews will also leave cuttings free for the taking.

willowy escape
right: **Elaborate and elegant, this willow bentwood structure offers welcome shade on a sizzling summer afternoon. Decorated with white lights, it makes a romantic getaway for candlelit dinners.**

best woods for bentwood

The choicest woods for outdoor structures stand up to several seasons of blustery storms, blistering heat, and blizzardy tempests. Long-lasting woods include cedar, juniper, arborvitae, bamboo, second-growth willow, and several kinds of locust. Woods with a shorter lifespan (one or two seasons) include elm, wild cherry, Oriental bittersweet, mulberry, mimosa, second-growth sycamore, ash, wisteria, and cottonwood. Grapevine also works well for outdoor structures, especially trellises or fencing, but it only lasts a season or two. Its naturally twisting growth habit can make it difficult to manipulate.

please fence me in

above: The tidy all-American picket fence takes a rustic turn when made with black locust trimmings. Drywall nails hold the pickets in place. Cut pickets so they stand clear of the ground, preventing moisture from seeping into the wood and causing rot.

rustic

tricks of the trade

Crafting rough, raw twigs and timber into stunning structures requires nothing more than imagination, a pile of wood, and a hammer and nails. Weaving wood together creates wonderful structures that appear to be rooted in place and part of the natural landscape.

Begin by seeing wood as a natural art form. Let each limb inspire your design; fit together the topsy-turvy angles and curves into strong, simple joints. A soft crook in a branch becomes a peak for

the view from here

right: To whet your appetite for woodworking, tackle small projects that give you a chance to hone your carpentry skills. Build a twig window box planter with a plastic window box liner. The liner helps prevent early decay of the wood and holds moisture for the plants.

branched passage

right: This gate would make Mother Nature feel welcome. Brackets crafted from apple and plum tree trimmings dress up the driftwood uprights. Fruit tree prunings, tacked onto a wood frame, form the gate.

a garden arch; a quirky V-shape twig provides a bracket for a corner joint.

Making arches and curved trellises or fencing requires pliable wood. Young wood is most flexible; bend wood as soon as possible after cutting it. If you wait more than two or three days, the wood will break instead of bend.

Attach twigs and branches with drywall nails. Use wire to reinforce nailed connections. Green wood dries and shrinks once it's cut, so tighten wires with pliers a few weeks after building your work of art.

hardwood haven
left: **Red cedar and mountain laurel form a gazebo and bench that look as if they sprouted from the ground. Peel bark from logs and apply a liquid preservative to the wood if desired. Otherwise, bark falls off eventually.**

garden decorating | **31**

romantic

love grows

Transform your garden into a fairy tale come true by filling it to overflowing with the accoutrements of romance: fragrant flowers, curving lines, and hidden corners.

As you plan your storybook hideaway, remember that the feel of romance thrives on what is unseen. Tuck a water feature into a shady secret-garden area so it is heard before it is seen. Enhance the mystery of your garden by granting glimpses rather than spacious vistas. Reinforce the theme with latticework, low-hanging limbs, and lush hedges that create peekaboo privacy. The effect should be neither contrived nor cutesy;

tie the knot
right: Use creative touches in your garden. A dwarf mondo grass love knot, complete with bow, trails along this stone walk, where turf wouldn't thrive in the shady passage.

instead aim for simple, charming, and captivating.

Typically, a romantic garden boasts an abundance of roses and old-fashioned flowers (sweet pea, dianthus, and stock) emanating with heady perfumes. Or a sedate green scheme of shrubbery, hostas, and groundcovers cushions a shady corner.

Romance is a state of mind, so choose decorative details that inspire a cozy feeling, such as low-voltage lighting or candlelight, soft cushions for snuggly seats, and water gently trickling from a pond or tabletop fountain.

great plants for a romantic garden

bleeding heart	lilac
clematis	love-in-a-mist
cosmos	oriental lilies
daisy	oriental poppies
delphinium	peony
foxglove	roses
heliotrope	stock
hydrangea	sweet pea
jasmine	wisteria

table for two
above: Transform a quiet garden corner into an outdoor cafe. Choose comfortable, sturdy furniture to bolster dining pleasure. This tiny table for two and folding chairs suit the cozy space. A brick floor keeps feet clean, making this a perfect spot for breakfast.

romantic

sweet mystery of love

Romance hinges on mood and the senses. Cater to eyes, ears, and noses with a garden that bursts with sense-appeal. Plants that promise sensory experiences include velvety lamb's-ears, lusciously fragrant lilacs or mock orange, and traditional love-me, love-me-not daisies. Papery-petal poppies and cranesbill geraniums glimmer in sunlight. Modest violets and lilies-of-the-valley suggest old-fashioned charm. Evening-scented stock and moonflower call to mind moonlit evenings.

Delight your eyes by establishing focal points, as well as vistas, in the garden. Place seating every 10 feet within any secluded nook. Focus on feeling when you select materials for flooring. Instead of using prickly bark mulch or jagged gravel underfoot, choose soft, treadable plants, including Scotch moss, blue star creeper, and Corsican mint, perfect for going barefoot. Curves, such as bed edges, fence tops, chair backs, and trellises, prove luxuriously alluring. Place them liberally throughout your garden.

enchanting entry

right: A beckoning bower and intricate iron gate exude romantic style. Victorian-era metalwork, with its curves and curlicues, adds forget-me-not style to any garden setting. To create a similar scene, establish fragrant climbing roses with heady fragrances at the base of your garden's portico. Great climbers include 'Climbing New Dawn' and 'Dainty Bess' *(shown)*, 'Zephirine Drouhin' (thornless), 'Blaze' (red), and 'Mermaid' (yellow; ideal for Southern gardens).

flair for comfort

left: A backdrop of shrubbery helps create a private getaway. Use fluffy cushions in pretty prints to encourage visitors to rest and relax there.

decorative trims

below: An eye for detail helps enhance a garden's ambience. White paint and detailed cutouts make this wren house a home.

nighttime escape

left: Evening strolls in this garden lead to a romantic spot, complete with twiglike steel chairs and a table. Grassy ribbons between flagstones stroke bare toes; flickering candlelight adds allure.

garden decorating | **35**

contemporary

no-fuss beauty

For gardeners who want high-style with low-maintenance, the contemporary look delivers both. Maintaining an elegant retreat does not require hours of care.

Plantings adorn the sophisticated sleekness of this contemporary garden (*right*) with hassle-free good looks. Mass plantings of a single beauty, such as ornamental grass, steal the show.

Materials for paths and patios display their durability in a neat, uptown look that needs only occasional sweeping or raking. Decorative details echo the uncluttered approach. A fountain, a privacy-providing arbor, and a modest clutch of pots represent sophisticated elements that personalize the contemporary garden with understated charm and unbeatable good taste.

grassy good looks

left: Ornamental grasses provide a nonstop show of color, motion, and sound. Their stamina keeps pace with the seasons, peaking from summer through winter. Care is a snap. Cut off dead plant parts in early spring, as new growth emerges. Divide clumps when they begin to wrestle for space.

surface savvy

below: For outdoor rooms near the house, choose easy-care floors instead of lush green lawns that require mowing, trimming, and other time-consuming chores. Use pavers or bricks in seating areas; combine concrete or brick flooring with gravel or crushed stone for pathways.

retire your mower

Maintaining a patch of emerald lawn might suggest suburbia at its best, but for gardeners who long to stop and smell the roses, the green grass of home isn't all it's cracked up to be. Consider various healthy alternatives to lawn that look good but take less time to maintain. Buffalo grass, heathers, sedums, sempervivums, and creeping herbs all make excellent groundcovers. For nonplant options, try pea gravel or a combination of cobblestones or pavers with gravel or low-growing plants in between.

contemporary

urban oasis

The goal of a contemporary paradise translates as "beautiful but undemanding." Begin your modern, modest-care retreat by establishing privacy with fencing, hedges, grouped evergreens, or vine-covered screens.

Find furniture that suits your budget and your needs. Place a roomy table and comfortable chairs in a dining area, for example. Site your getaway in a part of the yard that's easily accessible from your home. If you plan to entertain or supervise nearby play, set seating near traffic areas.

A small patch of lawn provides enough green to soothe and satisfy the eye. Surround the patch with a combination of low-maintenance plantings

easy elegance

above right: **Connect garden and deck areas with potted plants, such as Alberta spruce, geraniums, and plectranthus, which boast easy-care beauty. Enhance the scene's hassle-free charm with sleek metal furniture.**

a quiet corner

right: **Turn an unused, shady area into a perfect place for conversation with a neat floor and inviting seating. A covering of bright paint turns the chairs into the garden's artful focal point.**

and creative surface treatments. Use shredded bark mulch for low-traffic pathways. For seating areas, choose smooth surfaces, such as pavers or concrete. Mix stone treatments for a look that's aesthetically pleasing and natural.

For plants, focus on easy-care ornamentals. For height, count on vines: climbing hydrangea, bittersweet, Boston ivy, or Carolina jessamine. Plant sturdy groundcovers, such as ajuga, chamomile, creeping thyme, or Irish moss. Fill in the scene using tough-as-nails taller plants with seasonal staying power, including ornamental grasses, herbs, yucca, daylilies, coreopsis, hostas, and ferns.

secluded simplicity
left: **A parquet floor easily fits your budget when it's made from blue star creeper and colored concrete pavers. Maintain it with occasional watering and mowing.**

asian

garden refinement

In Asian style, the garden comprises the universe in miniature. Stone, water, and trees represent mountains, oceans, and forests. Fluid lines compose natural-looking asymmetry.

Each part of the garden, from plants and surfaces to art, reflects thoughtful planning. Fastidious attention to building and maintenance results in a clean, groomed look.

Simple elements inspire an air of serenity through their careful selection and

eastward passage

right: **A shaded walkway becomes a path to Asia with the addition of a traditional multipiece stone Japanese lantern. The stepping-stones and the arbor form clean lines, typical of an Asian garden. The subtle color scheme of grays and greens speaks of tranquility and peace.**

precise placement. This minimalist style lends itself to small spaces and limited time for maintenance.

The key features of Asian-style gardens take varied forms. Water trickles from a bamboo spout or reflects the sky in a still pond. Rocks appear as carefully placed boulders, selected for their artistry, set alone or as meticulously arranged groups.

Asian style emphasizes plant form and shape. Color schemes do not march through the seasons in brassy hues, but instead tiptoe along in subtle shades of green and gray. Occasional blooms or autumn foliage splash bright spots of color into the garden. Favorite plants include rhododendrons, azaleas, and Japanese maples. These species bear strong branch lines and welcome artful pruning. Flowering fruit trees, bowing ornamental grasses, and ferns provide other classic plant choices.

set the mood

left: For simplicity, bamboo excels. This bamboo gate, tucked in the middle of a white plank fence, proclaims this garden's Asian theme.

altogether asian

left: You don't need large spaces to craft a quintessential Asian garden because attention to detail seals the style. Stone plaques, a latticework screen, and iron chairs set the stage for this garden. A bonsai tree, a tea set, and thoughtfully placed round rocks whisper of the Far East. Potted plants, including Japanese maple, bamboo, hostas, ferns, and feathery astilbes, enhance the setting.

asian

beautiful bamboo

One of the strongest building materials around, bamboo includes a large group of fast-growing, graceful, and drought-tolerant plants with varied landscape utility.

From short to tall, light to dark, and tender to hardy, bamboo offers variety to bridge every gardening gap. Black bamboo (*Phyllostachys nigra*) and green sulcus bamboo (*Phyllostachys aureosulcata* 'Spectabilis') are winter-hardy, towering giants. *Fastuosa* varieties, planted 3 to 5 feet apart, form a living screen in three years. For striking variegation, try dwarf *sasaella* bamboo.

versatile display

right: Bamboo works hard in this garden. Split and whole bamboo form the fence. A bamboo waterspout plays a watery tune into a stone basin, flanked by a clump of yellow-green bamboo (*Pleioblastus viridi-striatus*).

bamboozled!

Look before you leap into growing bamboo. Plants spread by underground stems called rhizomes; running varieties spread more aggressively than clumping varieties. Use bamboo for erosion control or to make a living fence. Plant bamboo where it has room to grow or keep it in a container.

To curtail bamboo's wandering ways, sink a plastic, barrier-type container (which should be available at the same place you bought the bamboo) into the soil surrounding the roots when you plant the bamboo. Leave 1 to 2 inches of the barrier above the soil line. Fill in with soil, and then add 4 to 6 inches of mulch.

Use cut bamboo canes liberally in your garden. Tie canes to stakes or tepee-type plant supports, using twine. For fencing, gates, and other structures, use weather-resistant black polypropylene ties to connect and secure canes.

neo-traditional view
above: This garden blends Old World and new into a scene of sculptural beauty with its rose-covered arbor and traditional Japanese *koetsu-gaki* bamboo fence. Bamboo's long-lasting nature makes it an excellent choice for posts and fencing. Strong as steel, the canes' hard, outer covering repels water and resists rot.

tropical

tropical punch

Languish no more in the blasé, cookie-cutter lawn–shrub–tree landscape of suburban sprawl. Pump up your yard's volume with a touch of the tropics. Roll out a carpet of sensually textured plants, flaming tiki torches, and hot-pink flamingoes. You'll feel as if you've been transported to a delightfully exotic jungle (and the sense of a permanent vacation). Hang up a hammock and take in the tropics.

How long you'll enjoy the bodacious blooms of tropical beauties depends on where you garden. In warmer climes (Zones 7 and 8), transplant the tropics into your beds for year-round enjoyment. If you live in a temperate region, corral the wildness of the rain forest in containers and move them indoors before winter's chill arrives.

Select a tall, imposing plant (either in an oversized pot or in the ground), such as bamboo, abutilon, mimosa, or banana, for your sizzling paradise. Fill in around your selection with plants in a variety of textures, shapes, and colors. Cultivate an overgrown look by planting closely. Give houseplants an outdoor adventure by tucking them into your tropical landscape. The dramatic leaves of spider plant, purple setcreasea, and variegated snake plant provide bold color. The wonderful calypso look of crotons and Hawaiian ti plant, the sensual flowers of princess flower and canna, along with the sculptural foliage of fatsia and bromeliad also deserve a place in your tropical scene.

untamed and unrestrained
left: **The big, bold foliage of tropical plants demands equally flashy, substantial architectural partners. Recycled columns from a remodeling job resemble jungle-engulfed ruins when surrounded by cannas, bananas, and palms. A simple path in muted tones complements the textural tapestry of leaves.**

great plants for a tropical garden

agapanthus	citrus trees
bamboo	elephant's ear
banana	gardenia
bird of paradise	ginger
bleeding heart vine	hibiscus
bougainvillea	lantana
bromeliad	palm
brugmansia	plumeria
canna	princess flower

garden decorating | **45**

tropical

tropicalissimo

Fan the flame of the tropic's appeal by working touches of a vacation at the beach into your garden. A hammock or a hanging rattan chair will lull you into a world of tropical pleasure. Include pots of orchids around your deck or patio. The flowers linger lusciously. Clothe any patio paving surface with a simple sisal mat that feels wonderful beneath bare feet. Keep an exotic bird, such as a parrot, in a caged perch. Set up outdoor speakers, protected under an eave or camouflaged inside lightweight rock-look casings, and crank up the calypso music.

unmasked jungle

right: Water splashing over rocks or dancing in a fountain adds to a feeling of tropical abandon. Lush plants camouflage pond edging and enhance this garden's tropical look.

furniture finesse
left: Select accessories that fit the flamboyant flair of the tropics. Long-lasting teak furniture can't be beat for weatherability; look for environmentally responsible plantation-harvested teak to preserve the rain forests. Shorea wood is as weather-resistant and durable as teak but costs substantially less.

tropical trickle
left: Small spaces revel in the luxury of water. Search out a dramatic container to make a musical water garden. A simple, bubbling fountain creates a tinkling melody. Orchestrate a series of bamboo water spouts in graduating sizes to play a symphony of running water. Great plants for containerized water gardens include houttuynia, iris, lysimachia, dwarf equisetum, and dwarf papyrus.

eclectic

choices, choices

Most gardens boast
something of an
eclectic style. A mix of
details, acquired from
different places over
time, comes together
in the garden and may
or may not work as a
unified design scheme.
The eclectic garden
appears carefree and
personal, conjuring
a welcoming charm
in its assortment of
accessories, whether
new, homemade,
or hand-me-down.

If you make wise
choices and present
the elements of your
eclectic garden with
confidence, it's more
likely to work effectively
as a whole. With a
careful eye for
composition and
unity, you can happily

collector's garden
right: **A flea market
bench (repainted
green and rubbed
with a blue topcoat),
handmade ceramic
and tile mosaic
pieces, and mariposa
slate stepping-stones
from a builder's
supply store unify
this setting.**

include garage–sale goodies, as well as new features, to create a one-of-a-kind retreat.

While all garden design entails a journey of choices, the eclectic garden allows you to combine various styles, from classic to contemporary, in a single scheme. Repeated materials, such as stone, tile, or galvanized metals, work as unifying elements.

In addition, choose a dominant color, and weave it throughout the garden using plants, paving materials, and assorted accessories. Paint furniture, details, and structures, such as birdhouses, to tie together your color scheme. Use paint or stain to make new items look old.

garden art

above left: **This windmill was a flea market find at $65. The old watering cans make functional art; they're handy when the plants need watering.**

make a deal

Unleash your creativity to find good deals and decorate on a shoestring. Use these tips for bagging bargains:

- Arrive at garage sales and flea markets as early as possible.
- Go to auctions or tag sales on a weekday, when they're less crowded.
- When you find something that suits your fancy, negotiate a price.
- If you can't repair a rickety piece, plant flowers in it instead.

all-together

piecemeal peace

The all-together garden blends choice features in
a custom-look space that appears to have been
carefully created all at once. But the greatest
advantage of the all-together style comes by adding
items over time as your budget and energy allow.
The secret lies in gathering goods with a common
theme, such as a material, color, or pattern. Provide
seating the first season, a wall treatment the next
season, and some floor decor for the third. As long
as you follow the theme approach, any addition
will fit into the garden.

For a budget-wise, finished-look garden from
the start, focus on outfitting one small area at
a time from top to bottom. Complete a floor
treatment (to create the grass and paver
checkerboard, *right*, see page 58); then add a
couple of comfortable seats and a table. A section
of retired fencing forms an instant backdrop, and
a few substantial accessories complete the lived-in
look. Tucked into a cozy corner, this ensemble
boasts charm and affordability with simple themes.
As other sections of the garden join the decorative
show, a quick coat of white paint and black-and-
white striped fabric unify the diverse features into
a cohesive whole (see pages 52–53).

repeated themes
right: Repetition of colors (white and black)
and pattern (stripes or strong vertical lines)
ties together this and other areas of the garden.

lattice-back bench
above: A custom-made arch, featuring prefabricated lattice, transforms a bench into a garden retreat.

heavenly vision
left: Combine a classic garden icon, such as a concrete cherub, with boxwood and brick to create a formal look in any setting.

garden decorating | **51**

all-together

custom good looks

The appeal of an all-together decorative style
is that the garden grows with you; its decor keeps
pace with your own changing tastes and budget.
Many gardeners follow a collect-and-blend strategy
that typifies an all-together look. Creating
a garden that's alluring and captivating requires
attention to detail as you tackle the hunting-and-
gathering phase.

How do you blend flea market finds, tag sale
treasures, and fresh-from-the-garden-shop must-
haves? Try a few tricks from some of the top
garden designers.

color Buy paint in your favorite color by the
gallon at your local home improvement center
so you can make furniture, containers, trellises,
birdhouses, and other accessories the same color.
This unifies divergent styles and types of furniture
and art.

fence finery
above: **Repeat patterns of latticework
throughout a garden to blend separate areas,
such as planting beds and a garage wall,
into a seamless whole. In this scene, metal
fencing used to edge beds echoes and fits
the lattice theme.**

potting bench
right: **Include a work area in your garden.
A sturdy potting bench becomes a decorative
but practical work surface. This piece displays
a collection of antique terra-cotta pots on a
French wine rack.**

fabric Add cushions to your garden seating. Use fabric in a single pattern to link chairs, benches, and other seating options that reflect different furnishing styles.

architecture Sprinkle traditional architectural shapes (spheres, diamonds, or arches) throughout a garden to marry planting beds and seating areas. Latticework, which is affordable and versatile, unifies a garden with charm.

collections Display your favorite whatnots throughout the garden. Large birdhouses, concrete planters, or wrought-iron pieces are some examples of popular collectibles.

Tackle your gardening projects with tips and techniques from **www.bhg.com/ bkgardeningsolutions**

seating for several
left: An extra-large bench is a real find. Watch for comparable specimens at antique sales and church auctions.

warm welcome
below: Dispense with the welcome mat when your front stoop includes inviting cushioned antique wire French furniture.

structure

provide a framework

Arbors, trellises, fences, and other structures provide a framework for a garden, giving it form and enhancing its function. Structures help direct views, as well as traffic, through the garden. Structural components define garden areas, create a sense of enclosure, and establish the boundaries between your property and your neighbors.

stylish embellishments Coordinate garden structures with new or existing plantings and your efforts will transform a yard into a destination. Express your personality with your preferences for certain materials, colors, and details.

Where to begin? A clever floor treatment unrolls the red carpet of style, setting a tone for your garden. Lay a dramatic brick rug, a rugged concrete and groundcover patio, or a playful paver mosaic. Decorate walls with sculptural trellises or metal artwork and blooming vines. Use structures and surfaces to heighten your garden's sense of style, as well as increase its amount of growing space.

divide and conquer As you think about your garden space, mentally divide it into functional sections, such as seating areas, planting beds, and play areas for children or pets. Raised beds bring efficiency and symmetry to the garden, demarcating planting areas that reinforce the formal nature of the design. Deliberately place a flower-covered arbor to establish a welcoming transition from one garden area to another. When you add a screen, a fence, or a wall, use it also to frame an entry, enhance privacy, or hide an unwanted view of garbage cans or utility meters.

creative sparks Add a personal twist when establishing your garden's framework. Combine a need for seating with a passion for gardening by adding a rose-draped arbor with a built-in bench. Design and build your own fence. Personalize a deck with a painted-on rug, involving the whole family in the project. Salvage discarded building materials and give them new life, turning architectural trim into a trellis or chunks of concrete into a garden wall.

floors: grass & pavers

cost	make it	skill
$$–$$$	weekend	easy

you will need

- square concrete pavers
- spade
- porous weed mat
- sharp digging spade
- plastic mesh grid (optional)
- rubber mallet
- sharp knife

garden parquetry

Ribbons of turf woven through a hardscape surface break up what could be a large expanse of concrete or other uninspired material. The design looks both finished and refined but it requires little expenditure and initial effort.

First, measure the size of your area and figure the square footage of your desired grass and paver floor. Calculate the grass area by laying a few pavers (of the size and type you desire) on a flat surface, such as an area of existing lawn, and determine the width of the grass intervals between the pavers. Plan for grass squares the same size as the pavers or for narrower stripes. Use those dimensions to estimate how many pavers and how much weed mat you will need for the entire area. Use a spade to excavate sod and soil to a depth that will place pavers even with surrounding lawn. Line excavations with weed mat. Set pavers in place and trim sod to fill any spaces. Keep the sod watered until it's established

If you use this parquetry technique for a turnaround or an occasionally used parking area, lay a plastic mesh grid on top of the weed mat to provide extra support for the pavers.

elegance unveiled

right: **Capture the classic good looks of a formal garden with a grass-and-paver checkerboard. Mow the turf as you would an ordinary lawn.**

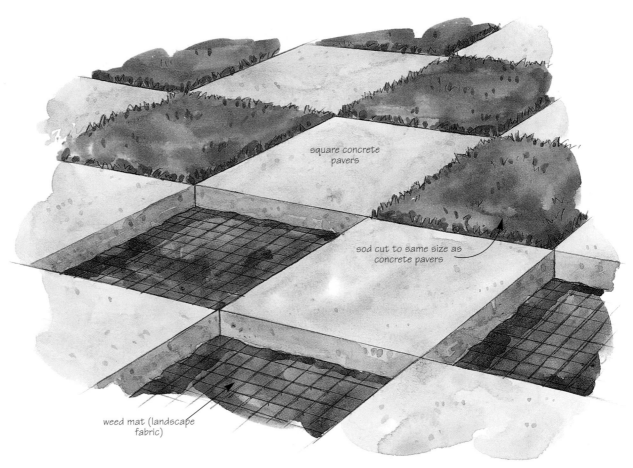

square concrete
pavers

sod cut to same size as
concrete pavers

weed mat (landscape
fabric)

harlequin lawn
above and left: In a
small yard, you don't
have to sacrifice
green space for a
patio. Enjoy both by
installing a grass-and-
paver floor.

floors: mosaic rug

fancy footwork

When dreaming up your garden's good looks, keep in mind that what's beneath your feet can also dazzle the eye. A mosaic rug for the garden requires no more upkeep than an occasional brush with a broom or a splash with the hose, but it rakes in bushels of compliments.

Site your stone-embroidered carpet in a prominent place: beneath an entry arbor, between garden rooms, or skirting a prized focal point. To reap the greatest enjoyment from your ground-level artwork, position the mosaic where it's visible from second-floor windows. Draw or lay out your pattern to size before breaking ground.

magic carpet

right and *below:* **Gather your mosaic materials from local sources, such as building supply or garden centers. Use leftover hardscape materials from another garden project. This pebble-and-paver mosaic measures 48 inches square.**

paving materials

1 3- to 5-inch river rock (100 pieces)

2 cobblestone

3 recycled clay street brick

4 Holland paver brick

5 Holland paver block

6 crescent Holland paver brick

7 handmade clay and mineral-glazed tile

8 peach and plum decorative lava rock

9 1-inch recycled glass

10 interlocking paver

To build a rocky rug, excavate an area
that's 2 inches bigger than the completed carpet.
Remove sod and soil to a depth of 6 inches in
frigid regions; 4 inches suffices for warmer climes.
Lay crushed gravel (4 inches deep for cold zones,
2 inches for warm); top with 2 inches of sand.
Snuggle stones and bricks into the sandy bed.
Start with the largest piece. To center a paver
in the heart of the rug, measure in from each
corner. Work out to the edges of the mosaic,
carefully positioning pieces.

Border the mosaic with cobblestone and brick,
leaving a 3-inch edging frame. Fill in areas around
stones with colored gravel and recycled glass.
Increase stability by sprinkling sand or dry mortar
mix over the finished carpet. Gently sweep the
stabilizer into place, brushing away excess. Fill in
the outside frame with soil; top with river rock.
The mosaic will settle an inch or two over time.

step lively
left: Create a
stepping-stone-size
mosaic using a
patterned concrete
block. Excavate an
area the same size
as the block,
adjusting depth until
the block sits at soil
level. Fill the block
openings with soil,
leaving an inch to
top off with colorful
recycled glass gravel.

garden decorating | **61**

floors: painted deck

custom carpet

Dress up a commonplace deck with a hand-painted rug. Area rugs easily anchor eclectic furniture ensembles and lay a foundation for an overall design scheme. Choose your colors carefully, and the rug you weave with wood stains and a brush or roller can integrate an outdoor living space with multihued planting beds.

First, determine how big you want your deck rug to be. Use a drop cloth or sheet to establish size. Then scrub the boards to be stained with a deck wash, following manufacturer's instructions. Let the deck dry for a few days before staining. In the intervening time, draw a design for your colorful carpet on a sheet of paper. Work with simple dimensions and shapes. Add curlicues or family handprints (or pawprints) to the design. Transfer your design to the deck boards using colored pencils, a T square, and a yardstick. This is a two-person job; all the lines need to be straight and square.

ready, set, paint!

Select your colors, using water- or oil-based deck stain, and begin painting. A tapered 2-inch paintbrush works well for this task. Use the colored pencil lines to guide your brush, since masking or painter's tape won't stick easily to the deck wood. The stain won't seep into the other colors, so work carefully to cover the pencil lines.

rug-making basics

right: **Build your outdoor carpet with blocks of color, much like a quilt. This rug features 6×18-inch rectangles arranged in sets of three to form six 18×18-inch squares.**

Let color blocks dry (about 30 minutes) before applying the next color. Paint the borders last. Ask a local paint store for recommendations on preserving the stain based on your region's climate.

outdoor floor coverings

Beyond traditionally drab indoor-outdoor carpeting, there are few weather-worthy floor treatments. Most don't hold up to nature's extremes of wet and dry. Woven rugs of jute, sisal, coir, and seagrass, especially those made from coir, can be a bit scratchy on bare feet. Place them beneath some kind of roof covering (on a porch or lanai) to protect them from moisture. If you want to enjoy them outdoors, it's best to do so just for special occasions. If you use natural-fiber carpets on your deck or porch, seal the wood flooring with weather-resistant stain to prevent damage from moisture that may accumulate beneath the rug.

finish the job
left: **Decide if you want to apply a coat of weather-resistant sealer. Without it, the colors in your painted rug will fade to muted tones.**

floors

paths and patios

Tending to a garden's floor transforms a lovely scene into a functionally fanciful environment.

It's best to tackle ground-covering treatments before planting. But adding paths through established lawns and gardens can be done. When trading lawn for walkways, select surfaces that dovetail dashing good looks with tough-as-nails durability. Bricks, pavers, gravel, and concrete top the most-wanted list of materials in landscaping circles.

Mix media to make paths and patios with one-of-a-kind looks at do-it-yourself prices. It's OK to blend bricks and gravel or recycled glass and concrete. It's also fun to pour concrete and

brick-a-brac

right: Red and black bricks laid in an angular pattern create a dramatic patio. Use soldier-straight rows of bricks to contrast and delineate path and patio areas.

abstract appeal

right: Concrete strips poured between sections of concrete-and-stone aggregate yield a sculptural, easy-care floor.

defined areas

far right: An orderly framework of bricks lends a formal feel to a path. Plantings soften the hard edges.

embed it with stones, tiles, or broken bits of china. Turn your creativity loose. Call in a contractor if you have an inordinately large area or a complex configuration, such as sharp turns or steep slopes.

Consider adding low-voltage lighting at the same time you lay garden floors (see page 174).

step by step
left: Laying an outdoor floor doesn't have to be the swan song of your lawn. Square pavers make a neat curved path across a former area of lawn. Now grass and clay meld in a catchy rhythm.

fences: custom pickets

cost	make it	skill
$$	2 weekends	moderate

you will need

two 6×6-inch posts; length: 56 inches long plus depth of frostline (A)

two 2×8×7½-inch post caps (B)

two decorative finials (C)

two 2×4s, 8-foot length for endboards (D)

two 2×3s, 8-foot length for rails (E)

five 1×4s, 8-foot length for spacers (F)

four 1×8s, 10-foot length for pickets (G)

scrap of ¼-inch plywood (for quail template)

router

water-resistant adhesive

zinc-plated screws and galvanized nails

premixed concrete

jigsaw or scroll saw

circular, table, or radial-arm saw

drill

hammer

screwdriver

exterior polyurethane or stain

posthole digger

picket pizzazz
right: **Merge fun and function by building a fence with shapely pickets. Develop your own picket design, using the quail dimensions** *(opposite)* **as a guide.**

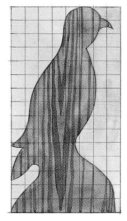

1 square = 1 inch

quail-topped fence

Pairs of quails keep watch over house and garden in this imaginative take on traditional pickets. Start with rot-resistant wood that stands up to the elements (cedar, redwood, or pressure-treated lumber). Posts should be rated for ground contact. The materials list at left makes one fence section 8 feet, 9½ inches long, including posts. Preassemble each fence section in your work area; then take sections outdoors and attach them to the posts.

make the posts Chamfer the four edges of each post (A) with a router (see diagram at *left*). For each cap (B), rout a 7½×7½×1½-inch square stock with a cove bit. Use water-resistant adhesive and galvanized nails to attach caps to posts. Drill a pilot hole in the center of each cap and screw in finials (C).

build the parts Round off ends and edges of two 2×4-inch end boards (D). Cut two 2×3-inch rails (E) 91½ inches long. Drill pilot holes and drive zinc-plated screws through the end boards into the rail end to fasten them securely. Make sure the rails are square with the end boards.

Cut eight 60-inch-long pickets (G). Enlarge the quail pattern (*above left*), transfer it to plywood, and cut a template for shaping pickets. Cut quails in pickets using a scroll saw or jigsaw.

Cut 1×4s to length and round the ends to form the five spacers (F). Nail pickets and spacers to rails, spacing them 1 inch apart. Help preserve the wood by treating it with an exterior-grade clear polyurethane or stain. Follow product directions for application.

fasten the fence Set and plumb posts (for more about this, see page 68). Drive screws through the end boards (D) into the posts to install the preassembled fence section.

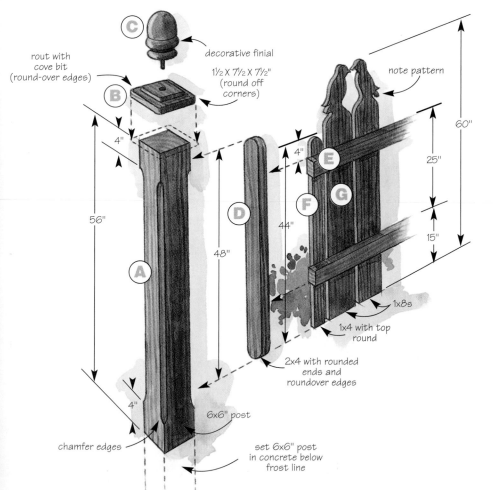

rout with cove bit (round-over edges)

decorative finial

1½ X 7½ X 7½" (round off corners)

note pattern

60"

4"

25"

4"

15"

56"

44"

48"

1x8s

1x4 with top round

2x4 with rounded ends and roundover edges

6x6" post

chamfer edges

set 6x6" post in concrete below frost line

4"

4"

fences

weathering heights

Understanding the basics of wood weathering,
will give your wooden fence its greatest mileage.

Moisture and the ultraviolet, or UV, rays that
make up sunlight are damaging to wood. There are
various ways to protect wood, each with its own
pros and cons. Clear finishes, such as varnishes,
water repellents, and penetrating oils, permit wood
grain to show. These coatings shield wood from
water but allow UV rays to penetrate. Add a
UV-filtering agent to clear finishes to slow the
sun-incited breakdown; renew the finish every
two years.

Oil-base, semitransparent stains alter wood
color while allowing grain and texture to show.
These stains don't offer UV protection, so you'll
need to recover wood surfaces every few years.
Semisolid stains contain more pigment than their
semitransparent counterparts and offer slightly
more UV resistance.

Opaque stains completely conceal wood's
natural color, much like paint, without covering its
texture. These UV-resistant coatings come in an
oil or latex base and need less frequent renewing.

fence post tips

Set fence posts in or on a concrete footing to
increase their lifespan. Pour a concrete footing
that's several inches larger than the post and below
the frost line for your area. Use bags of premixed
concrete, and set and plumb posts while concrete
is still wet. Taper concrete around the post 2 inches
above soil level to shed water.

for wandering eyes

right: A latticework fence allows glimpses of
the garden to passersby and gives a feeling of
openness and size to a tight space.

luxurious curves

left: Staggered pickets create a scalloped effect. Pair fences with bloomers, such as daylilies, miniature roses, or coreopsis, that won't hide the design,

good-looking gridlock

below left: A contemporary, 3-foot-square grid fence corrals a bamboo hedge and gives a greater sense of space. Smaller grids would add mystery and privacy.

wall treatment

below: A formal wall topped with a wrought-iron fence grants visibility and airiness to an enclosed space. Choose plants that arch and tumble gracefully through the fence, such as rambler roses, bridalwreath spiraea, forsythia, or honeysuckle.

walls: stacked-stone

cost	make it	skill
$$$	3 weekends	moderate

you will need

- rope or garden hose
- spray paint or flour
- wooden stakes
- pencil
- wooden measure
- string
- line level
- shovel
- flat stones
- sand

rock walls

A stacked-stone wall lends a distinguished air of character to even the youngest garden. The wall's course can be stacked several feet high, although most dry (no mortar) stacked walls run roughly 3 feet high, simply because it's hard to lift stones much higher than that.

Most municipalities don't require permits for walls under 3 feet, but contact local authorities before breaking ground.

If you're building to 3 feet high, the wall's base width should be 2 feet. For higher walls, add 8 inches to the base width for each additional foot of height. Most dry-stacked walls withstand some freeze-thaw cycles, so this building technique works in all climates. Choose stone at a local quarry; have delivery personnel place the stone as close to your work site as possible to minimize lugging. Because this project is physically demanding, spread the work over several weekends.

raised-bed planting

right: **Growing plants in raised beds offers many benefits: The beds are easy to work, soil drains well, and walls double as seating. Fill beds with your own soil mix rich in organic amendments, such as compost and rotted manure.**

1 design Plan the course of your wall using a rope or garden hose to define the bed shape. Mark the line on your lawn with spray paint or flour. To set the level of the wall, hammer stakes into the ground along the line. Mark the height of the wall on each stake. Connect the marks with a taut string. Use a level to make sure the height is even. Excavate turf and soil to a depth of 6 inches.

2 stack Add 2 inches of sand beneath the wall for a base. Choose the largest stones for the first layer, tilting them slightly down and back. Follow this tilting pattern for subsequent layers to increase wall stability. Fill the crevices between and behind stones with soil; stones should fit snugly together and not rock in place. Overlap stones, leaving no uninterrupted vertical seams running from the top to the bottom of the wall.

3 plant Place each rock with the nicest edge facing out. Use the taut string to guide your stacking efforts so that you build to the correct height. If your site is sloping, adjust the string's height to compensate for the slope so that the finished wall appears level. Finish the top of the wall with large, flat stones. If you want plants to grow from the wall itself, leave spaces between rocks to create planting pockets.

walls

building up

One of the longest-lasting decorative threads you can weave into a garden tapestry is a wall. A stone, plaster, brick, or concrete wall gives a feeling of permanence to even the newest garden. Use walls to separate garden areas, to add an architectural element to a single garden section, or to create a backdrop for flowers.

Stone, concrete, or modular masonry block afford the greatest durability and building ease; they're weatherproof, insect-proof, and maintenance-free. For a natural, stacked-stone wall, raise rocks to the desired height with or without mortar. Visit a local quarry or landscaping retailer to choose stone for your project, to estimate amounts needed, and to arrange delivery.

serpentine stones

above right: Walls don't have to be arrow-straight. Use a flour trail to plan curving lines. Fill pockets with shrub roses, such as 'Bonica' or 'Carefree Wonder.'

urban recycling

right: Recrete (used concrete) chunks stack neatly to form a retaining wall for little, if any, cost.

warming wall

far right: Put outdoor walls to work by using them to contain a fireplace or pizza oven.

Order more than you will need. You'll want extras from which to choose when building your wall. If you have rocks left over, use them in the garden. Hire professionals if your wall will be more than 3 feet tall because it will require footings and likely a building permit.

wallflower wannabes

No matter what style wall you choose for your garden, surround it with lush tangles of softening foliage and flowers. Some plants dangle beguilingly over walls. Trailers include sutera, brachyscome, candytuft, creeping veronica, sedum, thyme, alyssum, million bells, diascia, or dianthus. Dress up a wall with a petticoat of color, choosing bloomers that thrive in well-drained soil, such as arabis, aubrieta, campanula, *Geranium sanguineum*, and forget-me-not. Count on biennials, perennials, and self-seeding annuals to complement walls with towering flowers: foxglove, hollyhock, *Verbena bonariensis*, love-lies-bleeding, snapdragon, and flowering tobacco.

pick-me-up grid

left: Latticework panels add artistry to a blank wall and provide the perfect climbing surface for perennial vining plants, such as honeysuckle, trumpet creeper, ivy, and clematis. Morning glory, cardinal climber, sweet pea, and moonflower unfurl leaves and flowers that grow easily from seed for annual color.

arbors: traditional entry

cost	make it	skill
$$	weekend	moderate

you will need

four 10–foot 2×4s (A)

four 8–foot 1×4s (B)

thirteen 4–foot 2×2s or seven 8–foot 2×2s cut in half, or 13 precut deck spindles (C)

72 feet of lath or twenty–four 36–inch pieces (D and E)

approximately 60 3–inch deck screws

approximately 30 2–inch deck screws

approximately 12 1⅞–inch deck screws (for brackets; optional)

approximately 50 6d galvanized nails

3–4 gallons gravel

exterior-grade latex stain or polyurethane sealer (optional)

quick coverage

right: Choose arbor-enhancing vines, such as annual morning glory, cypress vine, or thunbergia, for easy color from seed that lingers until frost. Compost vines after frost.

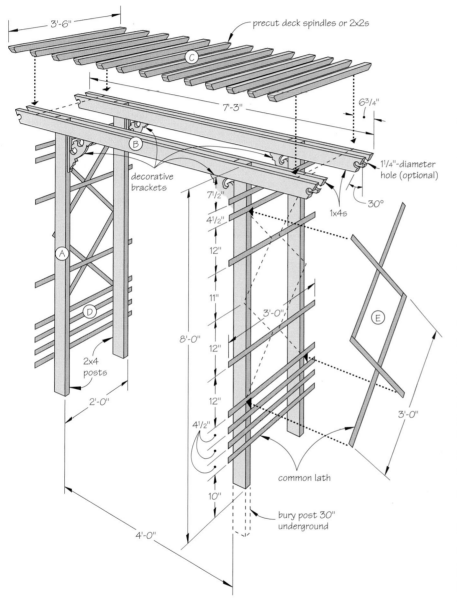

precut deck spindles or 2x2s

3'-6"

7'-3"

6³/₄"

1¹/₄"-diameter hole (optional)

30°

decorative brackets

1x4s

7¹/₂"

4¹/₂"

12"

11"

3'-0"

8'-0"

12"

2'-0"

12"

4¹/₂"

3'-0"

10"

common lath

bury post 30" underground

4'-0"

2x4 posts

welcome, friends!

The price tags of many arbors (even those made from kits) soar as high as the structures themselves. This plan for an entry arbor is affordable, elegant, and easy to build.

Begin with rot-resistant wood, such as cedar, redwood, or pressure-treated pine. Dig 30-inch-deep holes for the four main 2×4 posts (A). Add 6 inches of gravel to the holes for drainage.

Cut the four 1×4 top rails (B) into 7-foot, 3-inch lengths. To add the optional 1¼-inch decorative hole, mark the hole and 30-degree ends before cutting rails. Drill the hole with a 1¼-inch flat bit; then cut off the end along the marked line.

If you didn't purchase precut deck spindles, cut the thirteen 2×2s (C) to 3-foot, 6-inch pieces, adding a 45-degree bevel on both ends. Cut the common lath (D) into twenty-four 3-foot pieces.

sides Lay the four uprights (A) side by side on their narrow sides on a flat surface with the ends flush. Measure and mark lattice locations (D and E) on all four sides. To make each end section, lay two post pieces on the ground 2 feet apart. Nail horizontal lath pieces (D), attaching bottom and top ones first. After all the horizontals are mounted, attach the diagonals (E). Set the two assembled sections into the holes, plumb with braces. Fill the holes with a mixture of soil and gravel.

top Lay the four top rails (B) narrow side up; measure and mark the spacing (4½ inches apart) for the 13 top pieces (C). Attach the top rails with 2-inch deck screws and use 3-inch deck screws to fasten the top pieces in place. Apply construction adhesive at all joints to increase stability. If you're using decorative brackets, attach them using 1⅝-inch deck screws. Apply a coat of exterior-grade latex stain or polyurethane sealer, if desired, to help protect the wood against weather.

arbors

theme variations

Use arbors to frame a view, to greet guests, to provide a place for a bench, or to give the garden a sculptural feel. Arbors not only draw you along a garden path; they also provide a place for vines to scramble skyward.

Most often, people associate arbors with entry, indicating a passage from one area of the garden to another. Enhance this sensation with a little architectural sleight-of-hand. Intensify the demarcating effect of an arbor by expanding its borders. Add to the arbor's structure with

artful entrance
right: **A blend of cedar and wrought iron forms an arbor that's long-lasting and weather resistant. Use metal to incorporate curves into traditional right-angle designs.**

raised planters, built-in benches, or lattice-topped extensions (shown *opposite*).

Position surfaces underfoot to reflect the transition from one to garden area to another. A simple, affordable treatment entails laying brick or flagstone directly beneath an arbor and slowly fading it into gravel or mulch pathways on either side of the arbor. Decorate your arbor with annual or perennial vines that offer color and shade. For freestanding arbors, surround the structure with an abundance of lush shrubs, such as hydrangeas, shrub roses, and Korean lilacs, to form living walls and create a sense of privacy.

arbor art
above left: Gussy up a gate to do more than usher guests into the garden. Adding substantive concrete pillars, a top dressing of rail rafters, and a clematis vine creates garden sculpture.

rooftop creativity
left: With the posts of an arbor in place, turn your imagination loose and choose the covering overhead. This scrap-metal mesh lets the sun shine on the brick patio below.

trellises: circle-top

cost	make it	skill
$$	weekend	moderate

you will need

two 8-foot 2×2s (A)

twelve ¾×¾–inch lattice strips for crosspieces (B)

twelve ¾×¾–inch lattice strips for uprights (C)

twenty-four ¾×¾×1¼ inch blocks (D)

two 1×8s, 8 feet long, for circles (E)

exterior–grade wood glue

hammer, power stapler

4d galvanized finishing nails

carpenter's square

galvanized staples or brads

jigsaw

exterior–grade primer, paint, and polyurethane

two galvanized hinges, hardware

two galvanized hooks, hardware

handsaw or power saw

wall hanging

right: A handcrafted trellis looks good with or without vines.

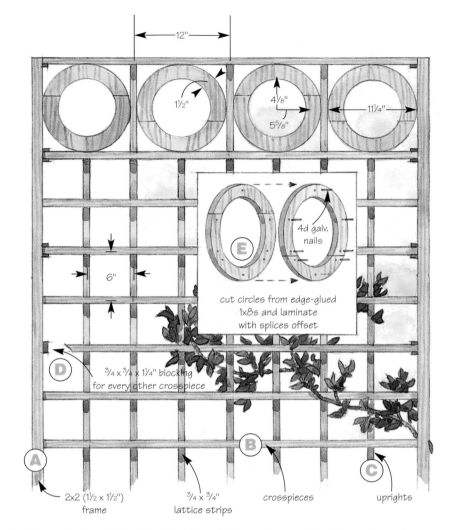

12"

1½"

4⅛"

5⅝"

11¼"

4d galv.
nails

E

cut circles from edge-glued
1x8s and laminate
with splices offset

6"

D

¾ x ¾ x 1¼" blocking
for every other crosspiece

B

A

C

2x2 (1½ x 1½")
frame

¾ x ¾"
lattice strips

crosspieces

uprights

builder's circle

For best results, choose materials of weather-resistant cedar, redwood, or pressure-treated pine. This trellis measures 6 feet high and 4 feet wide. Size your trellis to fit your site. The design works especially well to dress up a wall in a side yard or a courtyard. Train a vine on the trellis by positioning the structure over a planting bed or a container, such as a window box or an oblong planter.

Cut the frame stiles (A), lattice crosspieces (B), and uprights (C) to length, properly sizing openings for circles (E). Glue and nail support blocks (D) to stiles, spacing them 12 inches from center to center (see *left*). Lay out all the frame pieces on a flat surface and square them. Glue and nail or staple crosspieces (B) into place. Then attach uprights (C) to crosspieces, using the same method (glue and nail or staple).

Edge-glue the 1×8s together to create blanks for the circles. Cut them (when dry) into eight 11¼-inch-long pieces. Using a jigsaw, cut blanks into circles with a 5⅝-inch outside radius (4⅛-inch inside radius). Use exterior-grade wood glue to laminate the circles, face to face, with the splices offset. Glue and nail the circles into position between the lattice strips at the top of the trellis.

finishing touches

Prime and paint the structure; then seal it using an exterior clear finish. Or leave a cedar trellis natural to weather gray. Mount the trellis to the wall with hooks at the top and hinges at the bottom, so it may be detached if the wall needs painting or cleaning.

round up support
left: **An alternative design for skilled builders features a curved top and decorative posts.**

garden decorating | **79**

trellises: window frame

cost	make it	skill
$	afternoon	easy

you will need

- old window or door frame
- hammer
- nails
- 1×2s (optional)
- power drill/driver
- wood fence posts
- tape measure
- marker
- 3-inch drywall screws
- screw eyes (size 112)
- 20-gauge galvanized wire
- wire cutters
- seeds for climbing annuals

window treatment

Forget curtains and sheers. Dress up an old window frame with draperies of annual vines. This window frame salutes the day with sun-worshipping morning glories. Cardinal climber, cup-and-saucer vine, thunbergia, and hyacinth bean provide similar eye-catching results.

This vintage window frame, salvaged from a church, provides height and substantive architectural trims for this one-of-a-kind trellis. You could also use a door frame or start from scratch by building a custom frame using new trim and molding. Consider where you will situate this trellis in your garden. Attach it to an existing fence or to wooden posts using drywall screws. Make this a garden decorating project for the whole family, from the construction to planting the seeds.

all dressed up

right: A vintage window frame makes an upstanding garden feature or a screen. Multicolor morning glories eventually envelop the statuesque trellis.

1 reinforce Move your window frame to a work surface that's level and accessible from all sides. If you use architectural salvage for the frame, consider reinforcing it. You don't want the structure to wobble when it's upright in the garden and exposed to wind. Brace the frame by nailing 1×2s over all the joints and possibly along the entire length of the back. This frame was three-sided to begin with; nailing a 1×4 across the bottom strengthened the structure.

2 measure Starting at the top of the frame and, working down, measure and mark 6-inch increments along the inside edge of the frame. These are the points where you'll insert screw eyes. Do this on all four sides of the frame. Predrill pilot holes at each mark, and then twist the screw eyes into place.

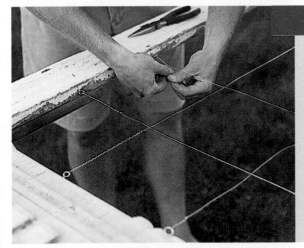

3 wire Position vertical wires first by looping wire through the first screw eye at the top left. Twist the wire to secure it, and then pull it taut to the corresponding eye at the bottom. Add 10 inches to the wire's length; clip and then twist the excess length to secure it. Repeat the process until all vertical wires are in place. To create horizontal rows, start at one side and weave wire over and under vertical rows to the opposite eye. Secure the wire ends.

garden decorating | **81**

trellises: vine poles

cost	make it	skill
$	1 day	moderate

you will need

- three 8-foot 1×4s
- two 6-foot 1×2s
- compass
- band saw or jigsaw
- 120-grit sandpaper
- weatherproof wood glue
- 3d (1¼-inch) galvanized finishing nails
- power drill
- exterior paint or stain
- posthole digger
- shovel

tower of flowers

Planting a pole for climbing vines will reward you with a handsome column of colorful blooms.

Build the pole with weather-resistant wood. Cut 24-inch crossbars using 1×2s. Mark curved ends with a compass; cut ends with a band saw or jigsaw. Smooth the ends using sandpaper. Cut a 1×4 into spacers for the middle layer of the pole: one 9¼ inches long, five 8½ inches long, and one 35¼ inches long.

On a flat surface, position the 9¼-inch spacer flush with the top of a 1×4, aligning edges. Fasten pieces face-to-face with weatherproof glue and finishing nails. Place a crossbar against the bottom of the top spacer, centering it end to end. Glue and nail it into position. Repeat this process with remaining spacers and crossbars. Glue and nail the final 1×4 face-to-face to complete the pole.

Cut and sand the curve at the top of the vine pole. Drill a 1-inch diameter hole through the curved top. Seal the pole using exterior paint or stain. Dig a 30-inch-deep posthole, adding 6 inches of gravel for drainage. Have someone hold the post plumb as you backfill the hole.

blooming skyscraper

right: Annual vines started from seed, such as thunbergia, or black-eyed Susan vine, grow up where space is at a premium.

1×4"

1×2"

8½"
spacing

8' -long
4×4" post

2' -long
1×2" crossbar

7½"
spacing

1½×¾" dado
(groove)

signpost pole

Once annual vines break through soil, they reach for the sky. This alternative version of the vine pole features crosspieces poised on varying sides of a post and represents an easier building project. Mark vines' growth with imaginative signs painted on crosspieces of the pole, if you like. Involve the whole family in this project, inviting everyone to contribute their favorite locations (include distances from home to there) for a sign. Build the pole using an 8-foot-long 4×4 made from weather-resistant lumber with 1×2s as crossbars. Add names and mileage to the signs using acrylic paint sealed with a clear varnish.

great vines for climbing

bottle gourd	cypress vine	purple bell vine
canary creeper	hyacinth bean	spanish flag
climbing nasturtium	love-in-a-puff	sweet pea
climbing snapdragon	moonflower	thunbergia
cup-and-saucer vine	morning glory	variegated hops

trellises: wall trellis

cost	make it	skill
$$	one day	moderate

you will need

- two 23-inch-long 2×4s
- three 8-foot-long 1×4s
- 2-inch deck screws
- 1¼-inch deck screws
- ½-inch roofing nails
- exterior-grade wood glue
- 30 feet of 14-gauge solid bare copper electrical wire
- circular saw or table saw
- posthole digger
- shovel
- gravel

high-wire act

Cultivate living wallpaper by training a flowering vine up a trellis mounted against a wall. The result: a wall treatment that's lively as well as artistic since blossoms beckon bees and butterflies.

Use rot-resistant wood, such as cedar or pressure-treated pine, to give your trellis durability. Use exterior-grade stain or primer and paint to protect your trellis. Painting before you assemble pieces will spare you brushwork later.

Cut decorative grooves into the front faces of 1×4 posts using a table saw or circular saw with a rip guide. Cut a 2×4 to length for one of the upper and the lower cap; notch them with a jigsaw. Cut upper and lower rails from 1×4 stock, then rip the upper rail to 2½ inches wide.

pillar for plants
above: **A formal-looking trellis helps morning glories rise and shine, spreading their color across a drab wall.**

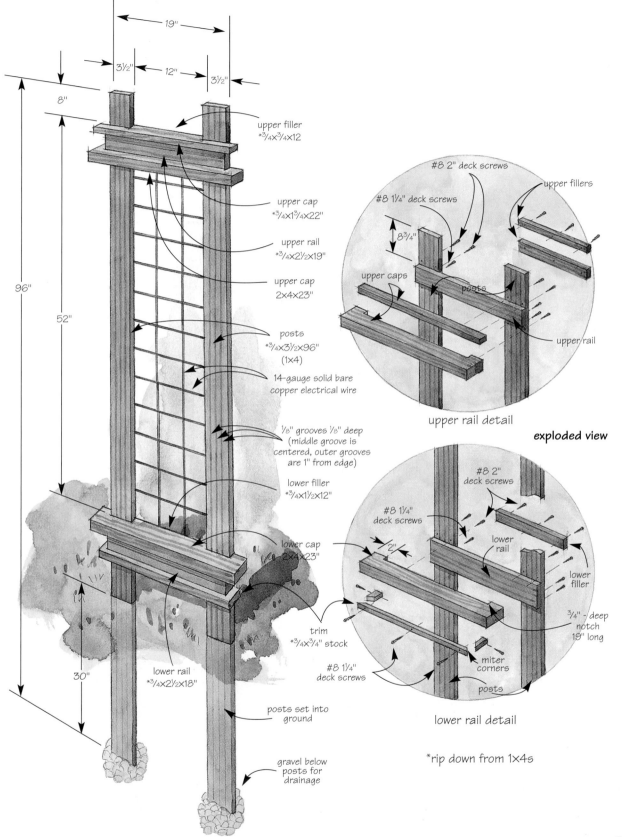

19"

3½" — 12" — 3½"

8"

upper filler
*³/₄×³/₄×12"

upper cap
*³/₄×1³/₄×22"

upper rail
*³/₄×2½"×19"

upper cap
2×4×23"

96"

52"

posts
*³/₄×3½"×96"
(1×4)

14-gauge solid bare
copper electrical wire

⅛" grooves ⅛" deep
(middle groove is
centered, outer grooves
are 1" from edge)

lower filler
*³/₄×1½"×12"

lower cap
2×4×23"

trim
*³/₄×³/₄" stock

lower rail
*³/₄×2½"×18"

posts set into
ground

30"

gravel below
posts for
drainage

upper rail detail

#8 2" deck screws

#8 1¼" deck screws

upper fillers

8¾"

upper caps

posts

upper rail

exploded view

lower rail detail

#8 2"
deck screws

#8 1¼"
deck screws

lower
rail

lower
filler

2"

¾" - deep
notch
19" long

miter
corners

#8 1¼"
deck screws

posts

*rip down from 1×4s

putting it together

Assemble posts, rails, and caps as shown (*left*). Fasten wood with weatherproof wood glue and deck screws (see diagram for screw size), driving screws from the back side of the trellis. Cut the ³/₄×1³/₄ upper cap, and upper and lower fillers, and trim to size. Glue and screw parts into position.

Place trellis face-down. Partially drive ½-inch roofing nails around the perimeter of the opening every 4 inches. Secure the wire end to an upper rail nail; loop the wire end twice around the nail and then wrap it around itself. Take the wire to a nail in the lower cap. Pull the wire taut enough only to straighten it. Loop each vertical wire once or twice around each nail. Then repeat the process for the horizontal wires.

Dig 30-inch deep postholes, filling the bottom with gravel. Plum the posts; backfill.

garden decorating | **85**

trellises

up, up, and away

Trellises take gardening to new heights without gobbling precious garden real estate. Start your vertical garden with annual climbers. It's as easy as pressing a few seeds into soil. Once vines climb the trellis, they'll continue reaching skyward. Annual climbers live life to the fullest in one growing season, flowering furiously until frost. All these high-rise beauties require is a steady support.

The type of support you provide depends on the plant. Twining vines (morning glory, thunbergia, hyacinth bean) wind along any straight support, such as latticework or bamboo poles. Tendriled climbers (sweet peas, cypress vine, cup-and-saucer vine) produce tiny stems that latch onto supports. They shin their way up best on mesh or strings.

luxury in bloom

right: When choosing vines for trellises, consider if the plants will be viewed up close. 'Ville de Lyon' clematis *(shown)*, shows off velvety blooms. Choose passionflower, cup-and-saucer vine, or chocolate vine (*Akebia quinata*) for their intricate blooms.

copper beauty

right and far right: Build a trellis from copper tubing and fittings cemented with weatherproof glue.

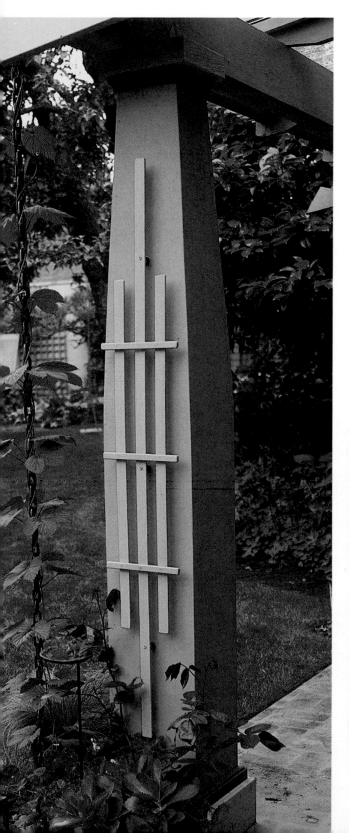

wall decor

left: Accent posts with colorful trellises. When painting wooden latticework, apply a coat of exterior primer first; then add color with exterior latex.

beautiful backdrop

below: Lattice sections create visual screens, as well as a home for vines or roses.

Perennial vines, such as clematis, trumpet creeper, ivy, cross vine, climbing hydrangea, akebia, and climbing snapdragon, climb this way as well, so select their support systems accordingly. The prickles or thorns of climbing roses don't help the canes climb or cling to a support. Give climbers and ramblers ample support, lashing canes to the structure with loose ties.

anchor away

No matter what kind of trellis you select, anchor it securely to the ground. The weight of mature vines easily knocks trellises down in a windy storm. Anchor slender supports (such as bamboo structures, latticework, or copper trellises) by driving concrete-reinforcing rods into the ground (either through or near the trellis); wire the trellis to the rods if possible.

garden house

a garden fantasy

A hodgepodge of old windows bound for the trash becomes a dream house for gardeners. The ultimate wizards of recycling, many gardeners specialize in taking what others consider castoffs and transforming them with creativity and elbow grease into treasures such as this enviable greenhouse (*right*).

A home–remodeling project and a similar structure displayed at a local garden show inspired the creation of this glass house. Follow this designer's lead. Instead of trashing replaced windows, compile them (or windows from a salvage store) into a light-filled retreat that's perfect for starting seeds, sipping lemonade, and puttering.

To get started, use our tips for creating your own garden getaway.

cover the bases

Site your house to face south, making the most of winter sunlight. If you live where mild winters rule, build a proverbial glass house using ground-to-gable glass, plexiglass, or plastic. In cold-winter locales, mount windows on a low wall to increase the structure's ability to retain heat. Glass or plexiglass are the best materials for a durable house in areas with strong or gusty winds.

Smaller spaces experience dramatic temperature swings. A greenhouse needs some type of ventilation to allow in fresh air and prevent the place from getting too hot and stuffy, which proves harmful to plants. Small, movable windows or vents near the top of the structure should suffice.

enhance the ambience
right: A garden house looks incomplete as a stand-alone structure. Surround it with plantings and decorative furnishings that complement its architectural style.

An 8×10 foot or 10×12 foot greenhouse provides ample space for starting seed flats and for storing frost-tender plants over winter, and it should not be hard to regulate its temperature. The climate of a larger greenhouse is easier to maintain than that of a smaller one.

simply charming

below: **Frame the house with a picket fence or a stone wall. Skirt structures with old-fashioned flowers, such as cosmos, hollyhock, peony, cleome, delphinium, and zinnia.**

glass-house alternatives

Easy-to-assemble greenhouse kits or prefabricated options make it easy to add a structure to your garden. Look for a size and style of greenhouse to suit the setting, as well as your gardening skills. Also look for an energy-efficient model at an affordable price (including the cost of electricity and materials to operate it).

The advantages of having a greenhouse include getting a jump on growing in the spring (start seedlings in a warm, covered area) and extending the growing season in fall (moving plants into the shelter). A greenhouse also enables you to grow a wider range of plants.

garden house

splendid salvage

Before building your glass garden house of discarded windows, take inventory. Assess the window sizes you have and then begin to piece them together, as you would a puzzle. The structure should be symmetrical. If necessary, trim windows to fit the design. Strip the window frames. Sand and paint them. Replace glazing that has cracked or fallen out.

Establish a simple foundation for the house. Concrete blocks work fine. Cover the blocks with siding, bricks, or stonework, depending on your garden's style. When positioning windows, suspend frames from narrow strips of wood set inside the house's timber framework. Caulk around the windows to prevent leaks. This building method makes replacing problem windows easier and is also safer in earthquake-prone areas.

For flooring, consider that gravel lets water drain into the ground below, whereas concrete is easy to clean. Raise the entrance above ground level for best drainage, and build a ramp leading up to the door; lay a flagstone or concrete apron just inside the doorway to make it easier to move things in and out of the house. Make the house's doorway and interior path wide enough to accommodate a wheelbarrow.

In cold regions, heat the house to make it habitable for plants during frosty periods. Provide necessary electrical outlets and adequate space for a heating system and a fan. Use rot-resistant wood shelving or metal benches to hold plants.

garden plans

Locate your greenhouse where it provides a substantial focal point. Traditionally placed in or near a vegetable garden, a glass house should be situated in a sheltered area away from shady tree canopies, low frost pockets, and wind tunnels.

air exchange
above: Plexiglass panels cut to size form the angular windows in the gables of this greenhouse. A system of levers and handles allows opening the top windows from ground level for climate control.

embellished entry
right: A salvaged door features a window-topped accent of decorative trim.

Once your garden house is in place, spruce it up with flower beds, blooming shrubs, or dwarf fruit trees. Add a patio outside the garden house to provide a place for relaxing between gardening chores. If shade is limited, create some with a trellis or latticework screen covered with a climbing rose or vine.

Learn how to make garden structures and walkways at **www.bhg.com/bkgardenprojects**

task-oriented

left: Plan the interior of your garden house with end use in mind. Shelves and storage are vital for seed-starting, as is a bin for holding soil. Hang tools on available vertical space. If you plan to overwinter garden equipment in the house, provide shelf space for that purpose. An interior water source, such as a spigot and garden hose, makes watering plants easier.

function

make it practical

The best, most functional items in your garden work hard and look good. Decorative elements often prove practical and even provide solutions. A trellis serves as a vertical focal point, as well as a plant support and a privacy screen; enjoy its architecture in winter when the garden ordinarily looks dull. Whether your garden decor provides comfort and efficiency or gives you more growing room and caters to wildlife, it earns its keep.

hardworking decor As you dream up fun ways to tackle the most mundane garden chores, you'll discover a world of practicality in bloom. Choose bed edgings, plant supports, and containers that serve their purpose and suit your garden's style. Select accessories for their artistry; they'll also reflect your taste and personality.

Examine your garden's decorative potential from a practical point of view. Consider necessities such as water, shade, seating, entries, and pathways; use the projects and ideas on the pages ahead when adding to your garden. See how stepping-stones (especially when beautifully crafted and creatively placed) entice you and visitors to enter and explore the garden with greater anticipation. Turn a needed storage place for tools into a piece of garden art that keeps your gear within easy reach. Transform a beautiful urn or pot into a delightful fountain that attracts birds. When choosing decorative features for your garden, check out their maintenance requirements and weatherability.

garden escapes Choose garden decor that enhances your privacy and gives you a sense of retreat. Create a garden sanctuary with cozy soft-cushioned furnishings, surrounded by vistas of green and fragrant plants. Add decorative elements that make you smile. If you long for a fire pit, go for it, but be prepared to entertain more as family and friends will want to enjoy it with you.

Heighten the satisfaction you'll feel in your garden by building a seating ensemble designed for durability and many uses. Or get that swing you've always wanted but didn't have a place to hang; build a lovely pergola for it and turn the swing into a garden getaway. A garden that is both beautiful and functional will multiply your pleasure.

stepping-stones

cost	make it	skill
$	weekend	easy

you will need

- ceramic tiles or plates
- safety glasses
- hammer or tile nippers
- plain precast concrete garden stone
- thin-set mortar
- heavy rubber gloves
- large buckets or plastic bins
- 3/16-inch notched trowel
- poly-blend sanded tile grout
- trowel or large rubber spatula
- sponge
- soft cloth

art underfoot

Handmade stepping-stones add an element of signature artwork to the garden without costing a mint. Make our mosaic steppers easily and as artfully as you wish. Design stones in one color scheme, as shown (*right*), or blend a kaleidoscope of hues.

Start with simple precast concrete stepping-stones and decorate with broken flea-market plates, scrap or discounted tiles, marbles, pebbles, shells, or recycled colored glass. If you avoid sharp plate pieces or tile shards, this is a great project to do with children. Place tiles or plates in a shallow box and cover with a cloth to prevent shards from flying. Wearing safety glasses, crack the plates and tiles into large pieces with a hammer or tile nippers. Use care: you want shards, not smithereens.

tiptoe stepping-stones

right: Stones made from pieced tile and broken plates may become slippery when wet. Use caution when walking on them after watering, or rainstorms, or early in the morning when dew still exists. Surround steppers with gravel or decomposed granite to improve tread traction.

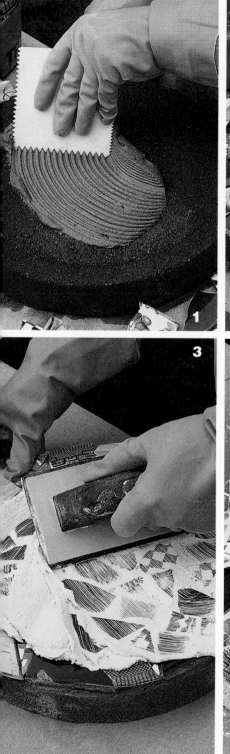

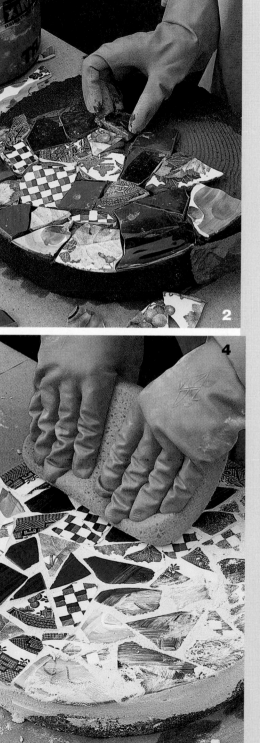

preparation Immerse the concrete stepping-stone in water; wet it thoroughly. Prepare mortar following package directions, aiming for a consistency of thin peanut butter. Use a notched trowel to spread a ¼- to ½-inch layer of mortar onto part of the stone.

1

artistry Arrange mosaic pieces to suit your fancy, pressing them lightly into the mortar. Work your way across the stone. Add mortar as needed. Slather it beneath thinner pieces to keep the surface even. Press pieces level but not flush; leave crevices for grout. When the surface is covered, clean any excess mortar. Let the stone sit overnight.

2

sealing Prepare grout according to package directions. Scoop a large blob onto the stone. Use a trowel or spatula to spread the grout, pressing it into crevices, removing excess as you go. Add more as needed. Smooth a layer of grout or mortar on the sides of the stone.

3

clean up When the grout sets (within minutes), use a wet sponge to wipe grout from the sides of the stepper and the top, rinsing the sponge often; wipe in both directions. Repeat this process until the surface is clean and fairly even; avoid removing grout from the crevices. Let the stone dry 24 to 48 hours, and then buff it with a soft cloth.

4

stepping–stones

trailblazing tips

The best garden pathways lead through hidden nooks and create a special effect too. Stepping-stones blaze the way as the simplest of paths. Designing paths is fun; building them, though also fun, is work. Tailor the amount of heave-ho according to your choice of path-making materials. Flagstones set among established plantings make for less work than a neatly edged path of carefully patterned pavers.

Stepping-stones offer a comfortable, appealing way to guide visitors through a garden. Use steppers for areas that are too difficult to mow or surrounded by established plantings. To set stones

walk this way
right: For a passage that's bordered with lush plantings, devise a path that's equally eye-catching to keep vision and feet moving along.

fanciful footing
below: Hand-cast your own whimsical steppers such as these, made with imprints of large rhubarb leaves on poured concrete forms.

in the ground, excavate a shape equal to the stone's dimensions plus ½ inch deeper. Cover the bottom of the excavation with pea gravel ½ inch deep to allow drainage. Position the stone on top of the gravel, adding or removing soil to make it level. Tamp soil around the stone. If you are planting groundcovers as part of a path, keep plants well watered the first growing season so that roots become well-established.

Involve the whole family in pathway construction. Set pavers in nontraditional configurations. Create designs on paper or with the actual stones in your driveway before breaking ground.

Don't forget night lighting. Paths that provide access to important parts of your yard should be well lit at night. Low-voltage lighting provides the best illumination.

flagstones go formal
above: Blue slate slabs roll out a welcome that's as formal as a black-tie affair, especially when evenly spaced and framed with neatly manicured grass. Edge a grass-and-stone walkway with bricks to make maintenance easier by giving mower wheels a place to roll without damaging nearby plantings.

a step apart
left: Surround steppers with earth-hugging plants for a natural effect. Mosses, creeping mint, blue star creeper, or creeping thyme fill gaps with ease.

paths: gravel

cost	make it	skill
$$	weekend	easy

you will need

- shovel and spade
- porous weed mat
- large stones, pavers, or bricks
- gravel or crushed rock
- wheelbarrow
- bucket
- steel-tined rake

stages of a path

Follow the steps shown on the facing page to make a gravel path, as shown. Alternatively, gardeners who are not in a rush can make a path on an easy three-year plan that won't break the back or the bank account.

In the first year of the three-year-plan, determine the path's location, based on existing traffic patterns and planting beds. Kill grass and weeds in the path's course by smothering them with wet cardboard (that degrades eventually) topped with 3 inches of wood chips or shredded bark. Frame the walkway with stones, bricks, or lengths of 4- to 6-inch-thick branches.

The second year, rake the wood chips from the path, replacing them with 3 inches of crushed rock or gravel. Renew and replace the edging with landscape timbers or bricks.

The third year, place 2 inches of sand on top of the rock. Set bricks, flagstones, or pavers on the sand, or pour concrete over it. Stamp a design or make leaf impressions in the concrete before it sets. Or add pea gravel to the concrete and brush it (while it's wet) to expose the stones.

fork in the road

right: **Divide large expanses of lawn or garden with pathways. A branching path leads to different destinations in the garden while creating a planting area between the forks.**

excavate Dig the path 6 to 8 inches deep. In cold climates, lay a base of 4 inches of gravel topped with 2 inches of sand under the weed mat (landscape fabric) if you plan to add flagstone, bricks, or pavers in the future.

Make the path at least 3 feet wide to accommodate two people walking side by side. If plants will border the path, add 6 inches to each side of the path. Use a rope or hose to lay out curves; broaden a path at the widest point of a curve.

edge Frame the path with large stones, pavers, or bricks to act as a retaining wall between walkway and soil that keeps the gravel in place. For straight paths, use landscape timbers. Lay wiring now if you intend to light your walk.

line and tuck Cut the porous weed mat to fit the full width of the path, following any curves and contours. Don't substitute black plastic lining for the mat; it will not drain properly. Do a little nip and tuck work on the weed mat along the path edges, pushing it under the edging. Cover any exposed mat edge with soil, gravel, or rock.

fill Complete the path by covering the weed mat with a 2-inch-deep layer of gravel. Smooth the surface with a steel-tined rake turned upside down. Backfill behind the rock edge with excavated soil.

paths

from the ground up

Once you decide to construct a path, create one that will be easy on the eye, the feet, and the budget. Focus on intended use and maintenance when selecting the path's surface. Gravel and mulch, although inexpensive, must be renewed every few years.

Gravel promises a crunch underfoot; mulch provides a cushioned walk. Flagstone dishes up durability that can't be beat, but it can be expensive and it's slippery when wet. Work small sections of flagstone into paths. Brick and clay pavers, which are durable and relatively easy to lay, inspire creative patterns. Choose bricks and pavers rated climate-tolerant for your region. Concrete and concrete pavers withstand any climate. For large projects, concrete pavers can be pricey, but interlocking types make installation easy.

country charm
above right: **Flagstones and bricks lend your pathways old-world enchantment.**

reward wanderers
right: **Focal points, such as benches or arbors, along your path will woo walkers.**

formal footpath
far right: **Economical landscape timbers set in the ground border a path of square stepping-stones and gravel.**

flower swirl

above: **Flagstones arranged in a staggered pattern set the tone for this easygoing garden. Ruffles of sweet alyssum soften the stones' edges. Positioning pavers in a purposefully casual, meandering line adds visual dimension to small spaces.**

piecing it all together

Planning a path includes a vital decision: What surface or building material to use. Take into account your budget, the amount of labor you're willing to invest, and the style of path you desire. In general, the more formal a path, the more expensive and time-consuming it is to build. Note: the following costs are approximate and subject to change.

The most popular footings for garden paths are decomposed granite and tumbled stones. Hot choices for garden paths include:

1 **Arizona flagstone:**
$239 per ton

2 **Tumbled Connecticut bluestone:**
$475 per ton

3 **Decomposed granite:** $50 per ton

4 **Three Rivers flagstone:** $415 per ton

5 **Concrete brick:** 50 cents each

6 **Black slate:** $475 per ton

7 **Eucalyptus mulch:**
$3.99 per 20-pound bag

8 **Connecticut bluestone:**
$445 per ton

9 **Burgundy clay brick:**
90 cents each

10 **Cedar 2×4:**
$8 for 12-foot board

11 **Tumbled Connecticut bluestone:**
$475 per ton

12 **Pea gravel:** $2 for 50 pounds

13 **Klinker brick:** 80 cents each

14 **Gold quartzite:**
$250–$300 per ton

15 **Iron Mountain flagstone:**
$290 per ton

edging: terra-cotta tile

cost	make it	skill
$–$$	weekend	moderate

you will need

- 12×12-inch terra-cotta floor tiles, ½ inch thick
- jigsaw and tile blade
- dust mask
- safety goggles
- mattock, square-point shovel, or trowel
- foundation sealer
- bucket
- mulch (chopped bark or gravel)

border treatment

Edging treatments are limited only by a gardener's imagination. Whether you use prefabricated edging or craft your own bed borders, you'll discover that edging, like fences, makes for good neighbors.

Our edging project begins with terra-cotta floor tiles, cut to a pattern, and tucked into soil. The tiles help foster a microclimate around plants, retaining the sun's heat near roots and promoting lusher, bigger plants.

English gardeners favor a trench edging for segregating lawn and flowers. Use this method along the front of a tile edge to make a mowing strip. Using a sharp square-point shovel or spade, dig 4 to 6 inches into the sod. Lift out the turf, roots and all. Clean the trench thoroughly by hand, removing rocks and roots, and then backfill with mulch (chopped bark or gravel).

tiling the garden
right: Incorporate floor tiles into the garden as bed edging. Turned on end and cut to suit your fancy, tiles keep turfgrass from invading flower beds.

1 cut Measure your garden beds and calculate how many tiles you'll need, based on using 12-inch-square floor tiles. On tile-size paper, design a pattern, favoring simple, fluid lines. Trace the pattern onto tiles using a pencil. Use a jigsaw blade designed for cutting tile to trim tiles into shape; wear a dust mask and safety goggles. If trimming tiles is beyond your confidence level, hire out the job. If you want to tackle cutting tiles but don't own a jigsaw, rent or borrow one.

2 position Dip the lower 4 inches of cut tiles into a bucket of foundation sealer to help prevent the porous edges from crumbling. Let tiles dry overnight. Use a mattock, square-point shovel, or trowel to excavate a trench for the tiles. Dig a trench 4 inches deep and 1 inch wide. Remove sod, roots, and rocks. Stand tiles side by side in the trench. Backfill to hold them securely in place.

3 corner Traditional edging keeps plants in bounds, but you can also use the technique to create a raised bed called a strawberry collar, which helps keep delicate fruits off the ground and makes them easier to pick. Dig a 4-inch-deep trench and set in cut tiles, securing them in place with soil. Add amendments to build up the soil inside 2 to 3 inches. For a permanent collar, mortar the tile corners and seams together.

edging

framing a garden

Ideally, edging should go in first, before plants, but incorporating edging into existing gardens is also possible. Use it to corral chaos, to keep things neat and tidy. But it can be beautiful as well as functional. Choose edging material to complement plantings, not compete with them. Edgings can be changed over time as long as they aren't set in concrete.

If grass borders your beds, select edging that gives your mower room to roll, or you'll be weed-whacking around every planting bed. Raised edging is charming. Three inches is eye-pleasing; 10 to 12 inches provides the right height for sitting. To groom a living edge, use low-growing flowers or herbs (sedum, catmint, or thyme).

favor your locale

right: **Think regionally. Gather shells, free for the taking, in seashore areas. Try them upended or laid flat for a 3-inch-wide barrier.**

angled for distinction

below: **Create a classic brick edge by digging a trench 4 to 5 inches deep. Add an inch of sand. Angle bricks into the sand, positioning half the brick above ground and half below.**

triple-edge bed

left: A gardener's itch for increased bed space can mean moving edging outward. The edging in this bed began with rounded river rock, but then an extension of creeping thyme was added. Curved metal bands came later to help separate the plants from the adjacent mulch path.

secondhand surroundings

Even the most expensive garden implements suffer damage over time. Instead of tossing your trusty tools, use them as garden sentinels, edging your favorite plantings. Cut broken tool handles to a length of 8 inches or less. Place them into the soil blade points up. Other fun edgings: On-edge broken clay saucers or plates, upside-down terra-cotta pots (4- to 6-inch diameter, painted brightly), or upside-down wine bottles immersed into soil.

garden decorating | **107**

furnishings

outdoor living

A gathering of furniture makes a garden more of an outdoor living space. When choosing furnishings, consider style, construction material (wood, metal, or plastic), and number of pieces. Wooden furniture offers durability and affordability. Consider building your own or hiring a local carpenter to craft pieces for you. The reasons to construct or customize your own furniture grouping:

custom designs Building your own furniture, using plans drawn up by master crafters or artists, means your ensemble will be unique to you.

affordability Choosing top-of-the-line materials to construct your furniture will help ensure its durability. You can select fabric and make your own cushions or have them made.

matching colors Stain or paint your furniture in hues that compliment and enhance your garden. Instead of an off-the-shelf red, try matching the blushing petals of your favorite lily.

ownership Building your own furniture multiplies your sense of ownership in the outdoor space you call home. A deeply satisfying sense of pride comes with seeing your handmade creation.

cottage casual

right: Simple lines highlight cottage style, and nowhere is that look more classically captured than in an ensemble of Adirondack-inspired furniture. An Adirondack chair offers roomy armrests and spacious seating; a tray table offers flexibility, with its detachable trays. A low table doubles as a footrest with hidden storage. To learn how to build this classic trio, turn the page.

cost	make it	skill
$$	weekend	advanced

you will need

- one 4×8-foot sheet ⅜-inch beadboard
- ¾-inch pine lumber (23 feet total)
- 1×2 (7 feet)
- table saw with dado blades
- table router with ⅜-inch straight bit
- jigsaw
- clamps
- masking tape
- pencil
- exterior-grade wood glue
- 1½- to 2-inch flathead phillips screws
- cordless drill
- bit for No. 8 screws
- ⅜-inch bit for plugs
- ⅜-inch flathead taper plugs
- ⅜-inch wood dowels

build a chair

Beadboard paneling adds to this chair's stylish look. Use ¾-inch pine lumber for frame pieces; ⅜-inch beadboard wainscoting for panels. Begin by drawing patterns (*below right*) on lumber. Use a table jigsaw to cut two of everything on the pattern grid, except for piece A. Label all pieces using masking tape and a pencil.

Join pieces using wood glue and screws. Use 1½- to 2-inch flathead phillips screws, except where noted. Throughout assembly, countersink screws that would be visible and fill holes with ⅜-inch flathead taper plugs.

Starting with the chair back, use a dado blade to cut a ⅜×⅜-inch groove into pieces A, B, and D. Join side pieces (B) to the top of the back (A). Apply glue to the grooves, and slip the beaded panel (C) into place. Attach bottom piece (D) to side pieces (B).

sit a spell

above right: **Adirondack chairs offer comfort in a timeless design that suits any garden.**

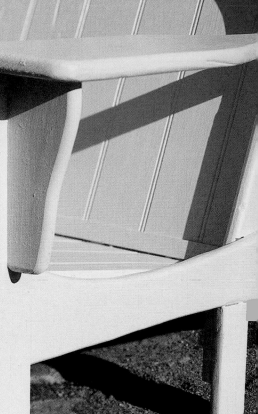

1 square = 2 inches

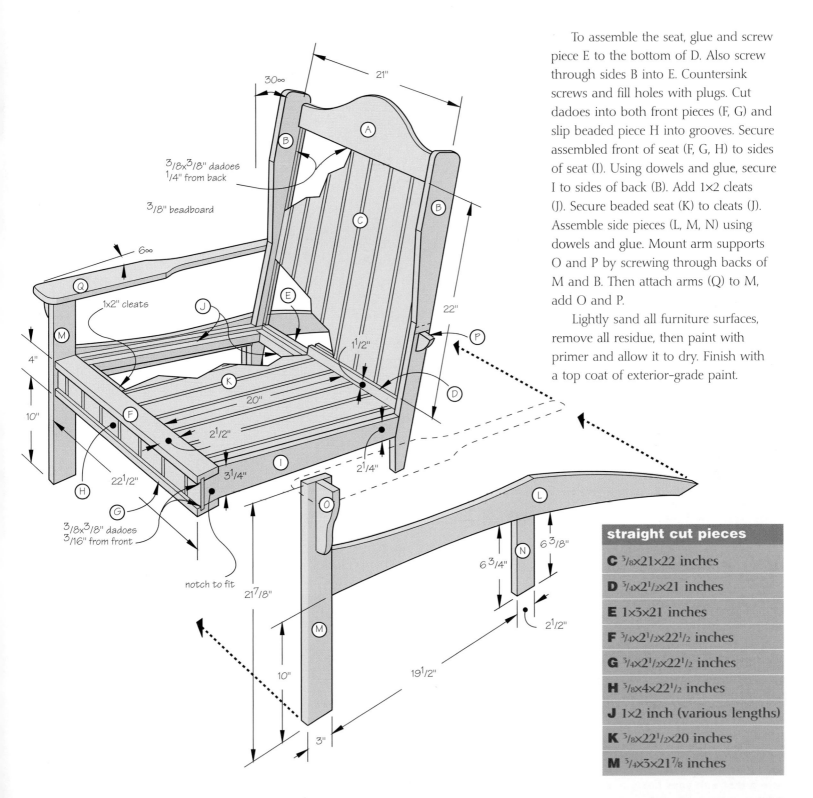

To assemble the seat, glue and screw piece E to the bottom of D. Also screw through sides B into E. Countersink screws and fill holes with plugs. Cut dadoes into both front pieces (F, G) and slip beaded piece H into grooves. Secure assembled front of seat (F, G, H) to sides of seat (I). Using dowels and glue, secure I to sides of back (B). Add 1×2 cleats (J). Secure beaded seat (K) to cleats (J). Assemble side pieces (L, M, N) using dowels and glue. Mount arm supports O and P by screwing through backs of M and B. Then attach arms (Q) to M, add O and P.

Lightly sand all furniture surfaces, remove all residue, then paint with primer and allow it to dry. Finish with a top coat of exterior-grade paint.

Diagram labels:

30∞   21"

$^3/_8$x$^3/_8$" dadoes $^1/_4$" from back

$^3/_8$" beadboard

6∞

1x2" cleats

22"

$1^1/_2$"

4"

10"

20"

$2^1/_2$"

$3^1/_4$"

$2^1/_4$"

$22^1/_2$"

$^3/_8$x$^3/_8$" dadoes $^3/_16$" from front

notch to fit

$21^7/_8$"

10"

3"

6$^3/_4$"

6$^3/_8$"

$2^1/_2$"

$19^1/_2$"

straight cut pieces
C $^3/_8$×21×22 inches
D $^5/_4$×2$^1/_2$×21 inches
E 1×3×21 inches
F $^3/_4$×2$^1/_2$×22$^1/_2$ inches
G $^3/_4$×2$^1/_2$×22$^1/_2$ inches
H $^3/_8$×4×22$^1/_2$ inches
J 1×2 inch (various lengths)
K $^3/_8$×22$^1/_2$×20 inches
M $^5/_4$×3×21$^7/_8$ inches

furnishings: stacking-tray table

cost	make it	skill
$	weekend	advanced

you will need

one 4×8-foot sheet of ⅜-inch beadboard (wainscoting)

1½×1½-inch pine stock (11 feet)

¾-inch pine stock (16 feet)

⅜-inch pine (18 inches)

table saw with dado blades or circular saw

table router with ⅜-inch straight bit

jigsaw

cordless drill

bit for No. 8 screws

⅜-inch bit for plugs

exterior-grade wood glue

2-inch flathead phillips screws

eight ⅜×1½-inch wood dowels

exterior-grade primer and paint

totable style

Use a table saw to cut all the pieces. Join the pieces with wood glue; countersink screws. Cover screws with plugs. Rough-cut handle pieces (G), and use a jigsaw to make the radius cuts and handle cutouts. Cut a ⅜×⅜-inch dado into all tray sides (G, H, J). Attach handle pieces (G) to side (H). Slide in beadboard (I), and attach side (J) between handles (G). Glue on pads (K). Use stock lumber and ⅜-inch beadboard panels to construct the table. Cut a ⅜×⅜-inch dado into pieces (B, C, E). From the tabletop, cut ⅜×⅜-inch notches out of each corner to fit table legs (A, F).

Assemble table by joining legs (A) to piece B, and then attach side pieces (C) to legs (A). Slide beaded panel (D) into grooves, and secure E to legs (F), and then legs (F) to C pieces. Finish the table and trays with primer; paint as desired.

fanciful colors

above right: A stacking-tray table has eye-pleasing appeal. Paint the trays in colors that suit your fancy and your garden.

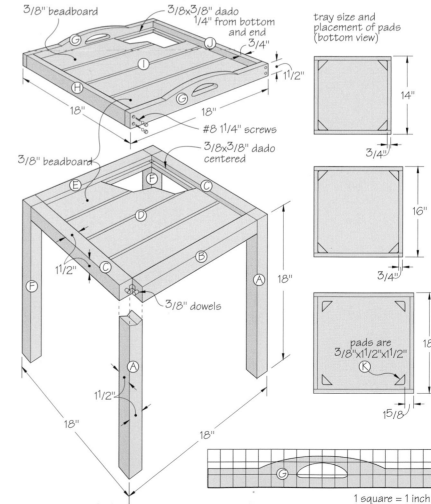

1 square = 1 inch

stowaway storage

left: This table is also a footrest that provides hidden storage. Use the compartment for stowing outdoor toys, or plastic serving ware and linens, or reading material, for days when you kick back and relax and nights when you entertain under the stars.

cost	make it	skill
$	weekend	advanced

multitasking table

Join the pieces with wood glue; countersink screws. Hide screw heads with plugs. Add a bit of glue to all grooves before sliding panels into place.

Use a table saw to cut the pieces for the footrest. Rough-cut the side-detail pieces (H, O); using a jigsaw, make the radius cut. Cut a $\frac{3}{8} \times \frac{1}{4}$-inch dado in top and bottom rails (B, D, E, H, I, L, M, O), as well as in legs (A, F, J). Cut a $\frac{1}{4} \times \frac{3}{8}$-inch rabbet in top frame pieces (P).

Assemble the base first, joining legs (A) to bottom rail (B). Slide beaded panel (C) into place. Join top rail (D) to legs (A). Attach bottom rail (E) between legs (A, F). Slide in panel G. Attach top rail (H). Follow same process for bottom with remaining pieces.

Join frame pieces (P) for the lid. Use wood glue and brads to secure panel Q. Glue and nail $\frac{1}{2}$-inch plywood bottom (R) to bottom rails (B, E, I, M). Attach the lid to the base with hinges.

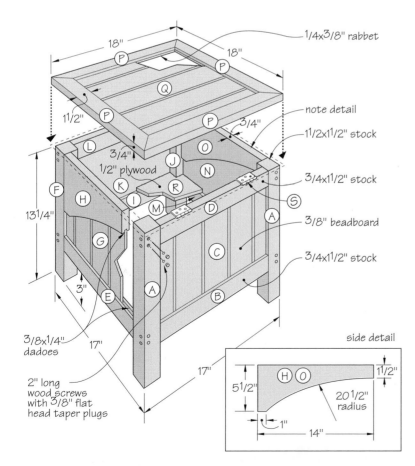

18" 18" 1/4x3/8" rabbet

note detail

1 1/2x1 1/2" stock

3/4x1 1/2" stock

3/8" beadboard

3/4x1 1/2" stock

11/2" 3/4" 3/4" 1/2" plywood

13 1/4"

3/8x1/4" dadoes 17" 17"

2" long wood screws with 3/8" flat head taper plugs

3"

side detail

5 1/2" 1 1/2" 1" 14" 20 1/2" radius

furnishings: bentwood & concrete bench

cost	make it	skill
$	one day	easy

you will need

- 2 side supports:
  4-inch diameter,
  6-foot-long branches

- at least 2 crosspieces:
  3-inch diameter,
  6-foot-long branches

- additional flexible
  6-foot-long branches

- wood saw and
  pruning saw

- pruner

- carpenter's square

- drywall nails

- concrete bench

- 18-gauge wire

- pliers

- hammer

- gloves

- twist ties

bentwood beauty

Weave a little romance into your garden with a handmade bentwood trellis that makes a pretty and practical addition to a garden bench. Start by drawing the design on paper. The bent locust creation shown (*right*) resembles a chair back and is fitted to the bench, which uses recycled concrete curbing for the seat and salvaged architectural structures for the legs.

Harvest wood locally, and bend it within a day or two of cutting, before it dries up and becomes breakable. See page 29 for the best woods for bending and building rustic structures. Support pieces should be at least 3 to 4 inches in diameter, while the more decorative twigs should be as thick as your thumb.

bentwood-backed bench

right: **Combine a trellis and seating to create a nook with a one-of-a-kind look that doesn't require a large garden. Start with a seat that suits your garden's style; then adapt the directions for this bentwood- and concrete-scheme to suit your plans.**

1 frame Every trellis starts with a rectangle. Lay two crosspieces over two parallel uprights about 3 feet apart. Square every joint; use drywall nails to attach crosspieces to uprights. Nails will drive through the wood and protrude on the other side. To avoid driving drive nails into your work surface, slide a board beneath the trellis. Do not trim nails until both pieces are attached. Last, trim off the crosspiece that extends beyond the uprights.

2 reinforce Secure a 6-inch piece of tie wire around every joint for added strength. Using pliers, twist the wire over itself. Because wood shrinks as it dries, retighten wires after a month. Bend the two thin ends of the parallel pieces to form the top arch of the trellis. Overlap the branch ends using 6-inch lengths of wire to hold the arch in place. Secure the overlapped branches and reinforce the arch by twisting wire around the wood at 12-inch intervals.

3 bend Always check the flexibility of a branch before attaching it. Complete your design by attaching all remaining twigs. The general rule is to nail wood that's thicker than a pencil and to use wire when one piece of wood crosses another. As you add lattice shapes, Xs, hearts, or other decorative touches, step back often to keep perspective. Use twist ties to hold curves temporarily, or enlist the help of a friend.

furnishings

seating options

Select furniture for your garden the same way
you would for your home. Choose pieces that suit
your taste, your budget, and your garden's style,
as well as those that offer durability. Your outdoor
furniture must contend with weather sometimes
at its fiercest, so don't skimp on quality. Start with
one piece or complete an ensemble, keeping use
in mind. If you entertain frequently, add pieces
that complement a dining arrangement, such as
a buffet or tea cart. If you just want a place to
perch between weedings, an informal bench will
do. Choose lightweight pieces if they'll be sitting
in grass and must be moved for mowing. Furniture
with classic lines easily overwinters in a sunroom
or family room.

armchair gardener

right: **Brighten the lawn, deck, or patio
with a cheery crop of flowers hand-painted
on chair slats.**

eye-pleasing pair

below: **Group garden furniture of the same
material. A rustic table and chair blend well
with a formal bench because they're all made
of wood.**

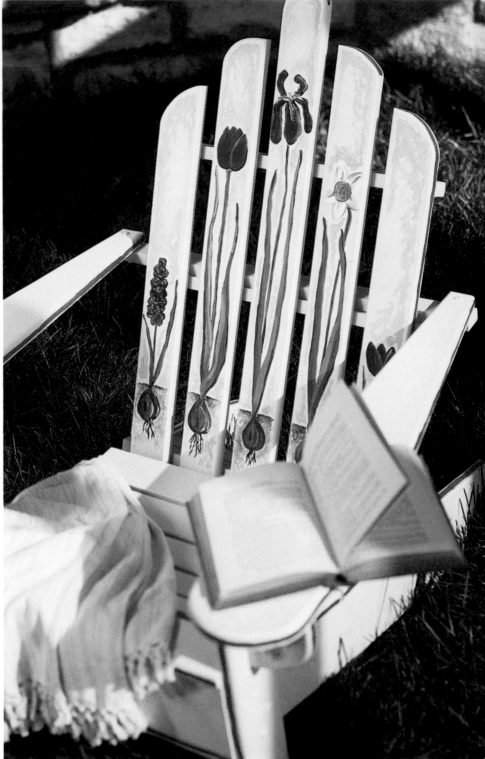

artistry unleashed

Turn your passion for posies into personalized seating with a few floral stencils, acrylic paint, and polyurethane sealant (*opposite*). Hand-paint original designs on wooden seats, or use stencils to get the look you want. The chair shown is outlined in green to suggest flower stems. A dry brush dipped in blue paint and patted on the surface creates a shaded look around the blooms.

To forgo fanciful flowers and simply paint wooden furniture, use exterior-grade latex. Rag-wipe wet paint to give it an instantly weathered look, or rag-wipe one color over another dry color to add even more interest. Seal with polyurethane finish, unless you want the chair to weather and peel (this process also occurs with a seal; it just takes longer). Check the finish each fall before storing furniture; reseal as necessary.

fabric finesse

Cushions made from fade-proof outdoor-type fabrics resist stains, moisture, and mildew. Unlike vinyl, these fabrics breathe and feel cool to the touch, even beneath a searing summer sun. Always bring in pillows that aren't weather-resistant; morning dew can ruin a favorite cushion.

lounge lizard

above: Weeding can wait when a lusciously cushioned lounge chair next to a lazy pond beckons. This vintage 1940s lounge exudes old-fashioned charm. Keep the period ambiance with cushions made from vintage fabric.

hard as a rock

left: A stone-enclosed corner and bench become a cozy getaway with the addition of comfy pillows. Choose heavy linen slipcovers that remove easily for laundering.

swings: pergola or arbor

cost	make it	skill
$$$	2 weekends	moderate

you will need

- 4×6s (two 12-foot, one 8-foot)
- 4×4s (three 10-foot, one 8-foot)
- 2×2s (eight 8-foot)
- compound mitre saw
- drill
- lag screws: (four ⅜×10-inch, twelve ⅜×8-inch, four ⅜×7-inch, four ⅜×5-inch)
- 24 flat washers (⅜-inch)
- ratchet set
- 90 deck screws, (3½-inch)
- level
- 4 bags premixed concrete
- 2 eyebolts (⅜×4-inches)
- 60-inch prefabricated swing
- 30 feet of ½-inch rope

carefree seating

Garden swings are all about relaxing, kicking off your clogs, and letting the breeze tickle your toes. Combine a pergola or an arbor and a swing to create an eye-catching focal point that also provides luxurious seating.

A swing requires more than firm footing. It needs sturdy supports set deeply into the ground. The structure (*right* and *opposite*) features 4×6 upright posts set in holes dug below the frost line. Both posts are held firmly in place with concrete from premixed bags requiring only the addition of water. Dig your holes larger than the width of the posts so enough concrete can be poured in to provide support. Choose rot-resistant wood, such as cedar, redwood, or pressure-treated pine.

swingin' decor

right: **Backed with a privacy fence and surrounded by fragrant plantings, this swing provides a pleasant retreat.**

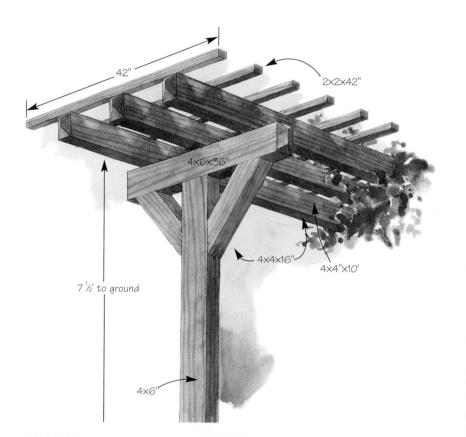

42"

2×2×42"

4×6×36"

4×4×16"

4×4"×10'

7 ½' to ground

4×6'

pergola construction

Start with the materials list, *opposite.* Make the following cuts: For the crosspieces at each end, cut two 3-foot lengths from the 8-foot 4×6; for the angled braces at each end, cut four 16-inch pieces from the 8-foot 4×4; and for the top rails, cut 15 pieces, each 42 inches long, from the 8-foot 2×2s. Then cut 45-degree angles at each end of the four 16-inch pieces to complete the braces. (As a decorative option, angle-cut the ends of the 3-footers and the 10-foot-long roof beams.)

On a flat surface, preassemble the two vertical T-sections. For each T, first attach one of the 3-foot 4×6s perpendicular to the top of one of the 4×6 posts, using two ⅜-inch-diameter lag screws, 10 inches long. Then attach the angled braces, using one 5-inch and one 7-inch lag screw at each end of each brace. Use washers on all lag-screws.

Then set and plumb each T-support in its hole (80 inches, center to center) and hold them in position with two temporary braces screwed to stakes in the ground. (Make sure both supports are the same height by laying one of the 10-foot 4×4s across the tops and checking for level.) Pour the premixed concrete in the post holes and let it set for 24 hours.

Finish the job by attaching the three 4×4 beams to the tops of the two end supports with two ⅜-inch-diameter lag screws, 8 inches long, with a washer on each, at each junction. Then, starting about 3¼ inches from one end of the 4×4s, use 3½-inch deck screws (two at each junction) to attach the fifteen 2×2s crosswise, leaving 6½ inches between each 2×2.

Hang the swing from two ⅜-inch-diameter eyebolts running vertically through the middle 4×4 beam. Suspend the swing with ropes or chains. If using rope, consult a guide to knot tying and find the three-strand eye-splice; this nonslip hitch holds most swings securely.

rope trick

left: **You don't have to be a magician to hang your swing with a cleverly placed rope. This supporting strand is laced through the swing's rear upright via a ½-inch hole drilled through the wood. Rope works well to suspend a swing in climates where harsh freezes don't occur.**

garden decorating | **119**

swings

rockin' in the breeze

Who needs a porch if you hang a swing in your garden? Once you begin to swing and sway, you'll discover how a swing provides one of the best ways to relax after gardening.

As you plan your swingery, locate a level place that has good drainage for the support posts and provides a relaxing setting. Site the swing where there's a pleasant view and plenty of room to rock away the hours. Surrounding plantings should weave a tapestry that's a joy to see, but keep greenery at least 2 to 3 feet beyond the arc of the swing.

from ceiling to floor

Swings beckon strongest when summer peaks, and they generate a breeze with little effort. Cloak your swing with a robe of shade to provide optimum heat relief. A lath house, pergola, or lattice-top arbor will cast cooling shade over your swing, making a sought-after retreat for sizzling days.

Tuck blooming vines or climbing roses into soil near support posts to add a little floral drama. A plant canopy increases the degree of shade and respiring greenery offers cooler temperatures. Include annual vines, such as morning glory and moonflower, to provide a dawn-to-dusk show. Trumpet creeper, cardinal flower, grape, ivy, and akebia are other good vine choices.

cool swingers

right: **Instead of hanging a swing from a ready-made stand-alone frame, create a setting. Build a lath house or pergola to cultivate a sense of place and permanence, as well as shade for your garden.**

Below the swing, place a surface other than grass, especially if you have children. Foot-braking the swing wears away lawn with only a few slow-down drags. Flagstones or bricks offer firmer footing that's maintenance-free. Pea gravel and mulch require occasional raking and replenishing.

flowery decoration

left: Top your swing with a living canopy, such as this clematis. Train the vine to climb and twine along overhead supports.

outdoor cradle

left: A hammock bespeaks lazy summer days, often spent snoozing as the hammock gently rocks. String a hammock between two trees or suspend it on a ready-made stand. Hang a hammock when you plan to use it; otherwise, store it to protect the fibers from weather.

plant supports: obelisk

cost	make it	skill
$	weekend	easy

you will need

- four 5-foot 2×2s (A)
- 14 feet of 1×2 slatting (B, C, D, and E)
- countersink drill bit
- protractor
- circular or table saw
- construction adhesive
- twenty-four 2-inch deck screws
- power screwdriver with No.2 phillips bit
- tape measure
- scrap wood and nails for tacking
- fine-grit sandpaper

eye-full tower

An obelisk forms a captivating pyramid that's every bit as fanciful as it is functional. Left unclothed with vines, this pointed structure serves as garden sculpture. Dressed in climbing bloomers, an obelisk becomes a supporting actor, holding aloft a bower of flowers. For vines with stems that wind upward (morning glories, beans, and thunbergia), push seeds into soil around the base of the obelisk. Press your pillar into service as a trellis for tendriled vines (peas, cardinal climber, and cup-and-saucer vine) by tacking fishing line onto bottom slats and peaks.

Build similar tepee-type structures from thick bamboo canes lashed together at the top with twine or topped with a decorative finial.

get the point

right: **An obelisk adds a structurally classic look in the garden, providing a place for vines to twine or serving as a focal point. Skirt your pointed tower with perennial bloomers that soar to various heights, such as these yellow coreopsis and pink bee balm.**

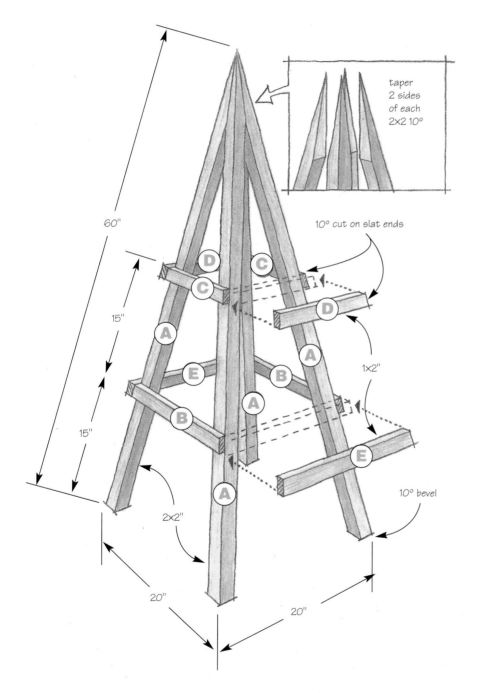

60"

taper
2 sides
of each
2x2 10°

10° cut on slat ends

15"

D C

C

A

D

E A

B

A

1x2"

B

E

10° bevel

15"

2x2"

20"

20"

aspire higher

Simple enough for novice woodworkers, this obelisk assembles easily in a day. Add another day to allow the wood finish to dry.

Start with rot-resistant wood such as cedar. Predrill screw holes using a countersink drill to prevent wood splitting. Mark 10-degree angles (on two sides) from a corner of the top of each leg (A) using the protractor. Make cuts. Lay two legs on a flat surface, apply adhesive, and press the pointed ends together. Screw tips together by driving one screw from the left through the joint and the other from the right through the joint. Glue and screw the two remaining legs in the same manner.

Measure and mark 15 and 30 inches up from the bottoms of the legs. Temporarily tack the legs together at the proper spread using a piece of scrap wood. Make pieces B and C by placing a 1x2 just below the marks on the legs. Mark cut lines on each 1x2 using the outsides of the legs as guides. Cut pieces to size and attach using adhesive, followed by one screw per joint. Then set both pairs of legs upright and screw them together at the top. Measure to make sure the spaces between legs are equidistant. Make pieces D and E by holding a piece of 1x2 against the legs. Use brace ends (B and C) to mark where cuts will be made. Assemble as shown using glue and screws. Bevel the leg ends so the obelisk can sit flush on the ground. Alternatively, bury the ends in soil until the obelisk is level. Smooth rough edges using sandpaper.

For a natural, weathered look (gray cedar), apply wood preservative or wood-tone stain. If you prefer to paint the obelisk, apply exterior primer first, followed by a coat of exterior-grade latex. After it's dry, tuck your obelisk into a garden bed and admire your handiwork.

plant supports: beanpole

cost	make it	skill
$	weekend	easy

you will need

- posthole digger
- 4×4, 12 feet long
- lumber scraps (2×4, 2×6, 2×8)
- four ¾×3×3–inch decorative pieces
- 2×4s (18 feet)
- sixteen 3-inch deck screws
- two 8-inch zinc-plated machine bolts with washers
- finial
- concrete mix
- 20 cup hooks
- heavy string

tower o' beans

Grow a beanstalk of fairy-tale proportions using an easy-to-build beanpole. This living skyscraper will win compliments. Plant edible pole beans at its base and enjoy harvesting blossoms, shoots, and pods for garden-fresh flavor all season long.

A beanpole adds vertical interest to a flat gardenscape, but it's not as permanent or as shade-producing as a tree. Best of all, its reach-for-the-sky attitude tames rambling vines into a neat and tidy tower, conserving precious garden space. Use the tower for other vining garden crops, such as cucumbers or squash, as well. This gardening technique also removes tasty sprouts from the reach of hungry rabbits.

beans for every taste

Celebrate the diversity of beans by planting several varieties on your pole. Select pole bean varieties only, not bush beans. In addition to the traditional green pole beans, grow some exotically colored ones for fun, such as 'Scarlet Emperor' runner bean (black and purple beans), 'Cascade Giant' stringless snap bean (green and purple pods), or scarlet runner bean (scarlet flowers attract hummingbirds). Alternatively, plant morning glory

top treatment

above: Dress up the top of your beanpole with a finial or, for a more functionally ornamental element, use a birdhouse to attract bean-beetle-eating birds, such as purple martins or wrens.

twining vines

right: Intermingle annual vines with stunning blooms, such as morning glories, moonflowers, or thunbergia, with your bean crop for more color.

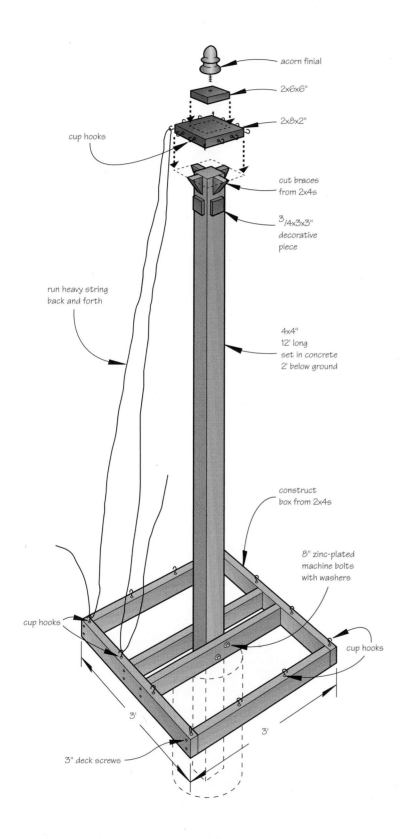

acorn finial

2x6x6"

cup hooks

2x8x2"

cut braces
from 2x4s

³/4x3x3"
decorative
piece

run heavy string
back and forth

4x4"
12' long
set in concrete
2' below ground

construct
box from 2x4s

8" zinc-plated
machine bolts
with washers

cup hooks

cup hooks

3'

3'

3" deck screws

seeds around the base of the pole and enjoy the tower of flowers that results.

build a beanpole

Site your beanpole where vines will receive at least six hours of sunlight each day and near a convenient water source. Using a posthole digger, dig a hole 1 foot wide and 2 feet deep. (Dig deeper if the frost line in your region goes beyond that depth.) Pour 6 inches of gravel into the hole.

Visit a local home improvement store to find a finial for your tower. If you want to stain or paint the finial, do so before attaching it to the tower. Prepare the pole's topper by squaring off a piece of 2×6 and a piece of 2×8. Attach the 2×8 to the top of the post, then follow with the 2×8 and finial. Screw cup hooks into the edges of the 2×8. Cut triangular braces from 2×4 scraps and screw them to the post and 2×8 to add stability. If desired, place decorative pieces cut from ³/4×3×3-inch lumber scraps on each side of the pole.

Set the post into the hole. Prepare concrete to a thick consistency and pour it into the hole to just above ground level. Plumb the pole and hold it in place while the concrete begins to set. Allow the concrete to set 24 hours; then build a 3-foot-square base around the pole. Screw cup hooks into the base (as shown at *left*) Run string back and forth between the cup hooks on the pole's top and base. Plant vine seeds in soil inside the base frame.

plant supports: live wreath on trellis

cost	make it	skill
$	1 hour	easy

you will need

- plants in cell packs or 2-inch pots
- cupped wire wreath form
- sphagnum moss
- soilless potting mix
- slow-release fertilizer
- floral wire or fishing line
- floral pins
- scissors
- disposable gloves
- garbage-can lid

ring around posies

Deck your garden with living wreaths. This circle of life dresses up the garden, hanging on an iron bed frame that transforms easily into a trellis. Hang wreaths in partial shade; water as needed.

go for the gold

right: **This wreath features a golden theme: yellow violas, 'Gold Child' ivy, 'Golden Fleece' Dahlberg daisy, and golden sage.**

1 gather materials Purchase a cupped wire wreath form at a crafts or hobby store. Choose plants in 2-inch pots or cell packs. Plants that thrive in wreaths include viola, alyssum, ivy, alpine strawberry, and small-leaf groundcovers. Select creeping or vining plants or ones with petite flowers. Herbs such as trailing rosemary, thyme, and marjoram also make pretty wreaths.

2 prepare the bed Soak sphagnum moss in water until saturated. Then squeeze out excess water. (Wear disposable gloves when handling moss.) Line the wreath form with moss; fill with a mound of soilless potting mix. If the mix doesn't contain a slow-release fertilizer, add it at the recommended rate.

3 add plants Pop plants out of their nursery pots, position them on the potting mix, and then tuck the rootballs into the mix. Fill in between plants with added potting mix and moist moss. Secure the moss with floral pins. Wrap the wreath with floral wire or fishing line, gently working your way between the plants and around the wreath.

4 care Use stout hardware to hang this heavy wreath. Water the wreath thoroughly before hanging it by soaking it in a garbage-can lid full of water. After hanging the wreath, check it daily; soak it when it feels dry.

plant supports: stake toppers

cost	make it	skill
$	1 hour	easy

you will need

- plant stakes
- toppers
- power drill (optional)
- screws
- paint (optional)
- all-weather adhesive

high stakes

Transform your garden into a gallery of stake sculpture by topping your favorite stem supports with life's flotsam and jetsam (most often found in junk drawers, craft closets, and workshops). Enjoy playing matchmaker by fitting doodads to stakes. If you choose objects that might hold water, drill holes in their bottoms so rain can drain. Attach toppers to stakes using screws or exterior-grade glue. Allow glue to dry overnight before setting stakes in the garden. Paint stakes or toppers, if desired, using bright exterior colors.

ramrod straight

right and *below:* **Decorative stake toppers reduce the hazard of sharp stakes standing unseen among leaves and stems, offering protection from an eye poke.**

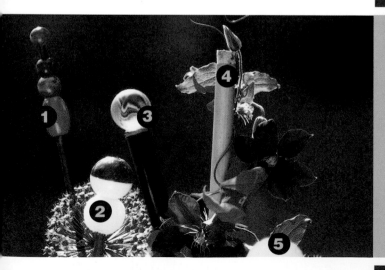

stake toppers

1. wooden beads on bamboo
2. plastic foam ball and fishing bobber on rerod
3. bouncy rubber ball on metal pole
4. cork, copper wire, and beads on plastic pole
5. plastic foam ball on rerod

stick 'em up!

above: A variety of stake toppers—a terra-cotta pot, wooden beads, copper wire and beads in a cork, a drawer pull, a watering can refrigerator magnet, a painted wooden pinwheel, and a plastic ornament—reach for the sky. Stakes include copper pipe, a closet rod, a broom handle, and plastic-coated steel.

pretty props

left: Almost anything can become a stake topper. A brass doorknob, a wooden finial, a pot of violas, a glass doorknob, and a large glass marble fit atop a variety of supports, such as bamboo and rerod.

garden decorating | **129**

plant supports: willow tuteur

cost	make it	skill
$	2 hours	easy

you will need

- 8 willow posts, 7 to 8 feet long, 1½-inch diameter
- 25 feet of 14-gauge wire
- metal macrame ring (or other type of ring), 18-inch diameter
- 50 thin willow rods, 5 to 6 feet long
- eight 1-inch brown ring-shank panel nails
- hammer

growing up

This twiggy tepee, known in garden design circles as a tuteur, arose from a French word meaning guide and instruct. In the garden, a tuteur guides and instructs climbing plants. But you don't have to speak French to make this classic design work for you. This willowy beauty uses tree trimmings, but windfall or prunings from locust, fruit, or cedar trees can also be used.

Begin by gathering eight willow posts. About 10 inches from the top of the posts, wrap 5 feet of wire around the bundle several times. Twist and snip the wire ends.

Have someone help with the next two steps. Space the posts evenly apart, forming a tepee. Insert the metal macrame ring inside the posts to about a third of the way up the form. Use wire to secure the ring in place temporarily. You'll remove the ring when you're done weaving, so don't snip the wire ends.

beyond the garden

right: **This twig-entwined tower blends the artistry of basket-weaving with a casual approach to function. Once you master the weaving techniques, create tuteurs of all sizes to fit large outdoor containers or serve as small tabletop centerpieces.**

Trim eight willow rods to equal lengths. Nail the base of one rod to the inside of a post just above the metal ring. Weave the rod over and under the next two posts counterclockwise leaving the end free. Nail another rod to the next post clockwise. Weave it over and under the next two posts counterclockwise, placing it just above the first rod. Leave the end free. Continue in this fashion until each post has a rod nailed to it. Repeat the weaving technique: One at a time, weave the rods over and under the next two posts counterclockwise, until all rods are woven. Weave eight more rods directly above this first section. No need for nails now; simply wedge rods between posts.

Repeat the process 20 inches above the weaving, using 16 more rods. Finish by twisting the willow rods to form a ropelike strand. Twine the willow rope around the tower until you reach the top. Tuck the ends into the wrapped-rod tops.

Conceal the top wire using a willow rod. Remove the metal ring spacer. Trim the post tops. Push the tower into the ground. Anchor it using a metal rod, if desired.

Plant towers provide a sense of height in the garden. Other height-inducing trellises include an old wooden ladder or a lamp post.

rung by rung
above: **Transform a rickety wooden ladder into an artful support for gregarious vines. Spin a little whimsy into the scene with a ladder-spanning spider web made from grapevine and attached to the uprights.**

timeless decor
left: **An obelisk, with traditional good looks, supports plants in style. Standing unadorned by greenery, the structure adds an outstanding visual element.**

garden decorating | **131**

containers

potted pleasures

Consider container plantings a stylistic part of your garden's decor. Match them to suit your mood, to highlight plants in their prime, and to transform an otherwise bare and boring area of the garden into a spot of color.

The mobility of potted plants gives them an advantage over earthbound plantings. A wheelbarrow, wagon, or dolly makes it easy to move pots, whether you want a colorful display: near an entry, in the shade, or in the limelight at an outdoor party. Master the tricks to creating gatherings that delight the eye.

choose a focal point Use an old wagon or wheelbarrow to make a collection of pots a focal point in the garden. Change the plants in the display as you desire. Protect surfaces; use pot saucers or pot feet under containers to prevent water from pooling.

combine container shapes Mix bowl-shape pots with ones that are tall and trim, broad or long. Set low pots in front, near the edges of container displays. Set taller pots in the back.

move them up Raise containers on pot feet, pedestals, plant stands, inverted pots, or bricks. Stabilize elevated containers to prevent them from toppling on windy days.

wagons ho
right: **Round up pots overflowing with pretty foliage and flowers into an antique wagon for a plant display that can easily be changed.**

roll 'em
left: Press an old wheelbarrow into service as a container caddy, loading it with pots of flowers.

portable color
below left: A collection of geraniums seems to bloom brighter inside a blue wagon.

focal point
below: Use a wagon to elevate a container and add a strong interest to an otherwise drab group of small pots.

garden decorating | **133**

containers

pot luck

Container gardens come to life in all sorts of shapes and forms, but the result remains the same: instant gratification. Pleasure abounds in a pot of colorful flowers that's easily planted and tended. Think of containers as accessories for the garden. Use them to personalize the scene, provide room for portable plantings, and allow you to grow plants you might not include in permanent planting areas.

Pressing vintage housewares and old garden gear into service as pots is fun and easy. Look for containers with character and room for roots to grow, such as an upended metal mailbox, a willow

a tisket, a tasket

right: **No need to throw away worn baskets. Line them with porous weed mat, fill with soil, and plunk in plants.**

cracked pots

below: **Broken bits of pottery and glass transform an ordinary container into a work of art. See page 97 for how-to information.**

laundry basket, or a rusted watering can. Plant in anything that will hold soil, from old drawers to a leaky tea kettle.

For containers made of cane, wicker, or metal mesh, line the interior with wet sphagnum moss, plastic garbage bags, porous weed mat, or an empty soil bag. Remember to poke a few drainage holes in the bottom. When filling wooden containers, seal the wood first (especially seams and corners) with several coats of a waterproof finish before adding soil.

All containers need drainage, so drill holes if necessary. If you prefer to keep the container intact, use it as a cachepot (that's French for "put the plants in a cheap green plastic pot that fits inside the fun container").

Use a lightweight soilless planting mix developed for container gardening. Mix organic or prilled slow-release fertilizer and water-holding crystals into soil before planting. Water plants whenever soil feels dry.

lush locks
above left: **Every day's a good-hair day when tangles of blooms form the tresses. This witty 'do unfurls in 'Elijah Blue' fescue accented with a tiara of daisies.**

seedy dreams
left: **A vintage seeder sees new life as a planter. Use antique pieces only if you don't mind hastening their deterioration outdoors.**

cloches

cost	make it	skill
$	1 hour	easy

you will need

3– to 4–quart glass mixing bowl

18–gauge wire

wire cutters

pliers

½– to 1–inch– diameter wooden dowel, 4 inches long

drill

spring fashion

Add an element of mystery and history to your garden by slipping seedlings under a classy glass cloche (pronounced kloash), the French word for bell. Gardeners have used cloches for centuries to protect seedlings and lengthen the growing season.

Make a cloche from a glass mixing bowl. Use bowls that are deeper than they are wide (old standing-mixer bowls are perfect). If the bowl has a foot, as shown, (*right*, at *right*) twist wire around the foot, leaving two loops opposite each other. Drill through a dowel from both ends, and insert a separate piece of wire through the wood to make a handle. Hook the wire to the opposing loops securely as shown.

For a smooth-bottomed bowl (shown on *left* side of photo at *right*), cut four wires the depth of the bowl, plus 6 inches. Bend one end of each wire into a 2-inch-long hook. Slide the hooks over the bowl rim at four evenly spaced points. Position the remaining wire straight up the bowl sides, twisting the ends securely together at the top, making two loops of opposing wires. Add a handle.

homemade hothouse

right: These old mixing-bowl cloches keep warm-weather crops, such as tomatoes, peppers, and eggplants, in cozy comfort as they get a jump on the growing season at least three weeks before the last average frost date.

cloche encounters

A cloche acts as a portable hothouse that raises soil and air temperature around frost-tender seedlings. Placed over young plants in early spring and late fall, cloches extend the growing season by several weeks.

The trick to using them is to remember how cloches work. They protect seedlings by capturing and concentrating sunlight, much like a greenhouse. On bright days, it's key to vent the cloche by propping up one edge (or even removing the cloche entirely) to allow heat to escape. Otherwise, you might fry fragile foliage. Cloches also protect tender shoots from hungry rabbits.

season extenders
below: **A cloche acts like a suit of armor for seedlings, protecting young plants from the vagaries of spring and fall weather. Glass cloches last longer than plastic ones.**

bird places

flight of fancy

Befriend birds with all the amenities of a guest house: a fresh bath and a comfortable place to sleep or stay for a while. Blending function and beauty, birdhouses, birdbaths, and bird feeders represent some of the most favored garden embellishments.

splish, splash

Birds will come in droves to take baths and sing in your garden when you provide puddles aplenty. Use professional birdbaths, handmade hypertufa creations, or terra–cotta or plastic saucers. Keep baths full and clean; replace the water every two to three days. Scrub baths weekly with a solution of one part bleach to nine parts water to protect your winged warblers from disease outbreaks. The sound of moving water attracts birds, so add a

bathing beauties

above: In a natural-look garden, a hollowed-out rock provides a perfect place for birds to sip and splash. Locate birdbaths in the open but with sheltering shrubs and trees nearby so birds can fly to safety if threatened. Ground-level baths appeal more to birds than elevated ones, although birds frequent any water source that's regularly replenished.

sheltering tree

right: A towering birdhouse pole does double duty by acting as a prop for a stunning vine, such as this 'Comtesse de Bouchard' clematis. Position birdhouses in or near trees to provide cover for birds. If you plan to train vines up a birdhouse pole, plant vines when you set up the birdhouse to avoid disturbing nesting birds later.

dripper or misting system to your bath. All you need is a water source to get dripping.

birdy buffet

While a diverse garden attracts birds with a variety of berries, seeds, and bugs, supplement the food selection year-round by setting out feeders and offering birds a varied diet.

As you plan your menu for the birds, choose feeders that accommodate the birds you want to beckon. Hang up a thistle feeder for finches, a nectar feeder for hummingbirds, and a roomy hopper filled with black sunflower seeds for cardinals.

Look for feeders that blend function with durability and good looks. Beautiful blown-glass hummingbird feeders sparkle in the sunlight like jewels. Copper and cedar bird feeders add a lasting element of beauty to the garden. Supplement any seeds, fruits, or nuts you set out with a healthy garden brimming with bird-friendly plantings.

cozy inn

left: **Add whimsy to your garden with a bird feeder that has all the charm of a country inn. Build a year-round magnet for birds with an enclosed platform-type feeder. For harsh winter areas, make it a house instead, including only one small entrance hole. Place perches inside for roosting.**

bird places

bird-friendly getaways

Hanging a birdhouse or two encourages birds
to set up housekeeping in your garden. Select a
house with decorative details, such as architectural
gingerbread trim, bright colors, or fanciful painted
designs, that will add eye-pleasing elements to
the scene but make no difference to the birds.
Be certain that the house you choose has been
designed for outdoor use by birds. Houses present
hazards to birds if they are painted inside, lack
drainage holes, consist of materials that cause heat
buildup, or have limited circulation.

    If you prefer to build a house, ensure that the
entrance opening is the proper size to admit only
the bird types you desire. Use scrap or salvaged
materials to create birdhouses with the charm
of folk art, but without the price tag. Start with

bird b-and-b

right: **Combine housing and food in one location
by attaching a platform feeding tray to a post
and top it with a birdhouse.**

victorian-style quarters

below: **Perch birdhouses on pedestals, porch
posts, or other sturdy supports. If possible, face
openings away from prevailing winds. Decorate
posts with fanciful woodwork.**

a basic plan for a house, build it, and then embellish it. Recycle sheet metal or cedar shingles for roofing, and extend the material over the entrance hole to protect birds in a downpour. Cut old shutter louvers to frame tiny windows; use leather strips for door hinges. Drill ventilation holes near the top back of the house, and attach the base or back with screws so the house can be opened for easy cleaning.

For information on birdhouse plans, contact your local county extension office, a garden center, or the National Audubon Society.

single-family housing
left: Because few birds will share housing space, equip your house with only one working entrance. Add other doors and windows for decorative purposes only.

in the round
far left: A birdhouse displays your building skills. Old moss-covered cedar-shake shingles find new life in this circular abode.

sturdy and stable
left: Give your birdhouse a firm foundation by mounting it on a wide, sturdy platform that attaches to a post at least 5 feet tall.

garden toolhouse

you will need

- assorted redwood or cedar scraps
- plywood scraps
- sheet metal
- ½-inch wood dowels
- galvanized wood screws, various sizes
- exterior wood glue

tidy toolshed

A tiny shed keeps hand tools tidy and at the ready in a nearby garden spot. The shed shown is 17 inches tall, 15 inches wide by 8 inches deep, but build your tool house with the dimensions that fit your needs. Materials for the project could be salvaged or bought new and distressed to appear rustic.

First construct the base; then build each component before assembling the house. The components include fencing, wall trellis, door and window, chimney, and interior hangers. Follow a glue and screw (or nail) pattern as you build. Glue parts together first; then add screws or nails. Assemble the house shell using plywood; then add wood siding. Next attach preconstructed components including fencing and other details. Attach the shed squarely to the base; then screw plywood into place for a roof. Nail sheet metal in place last.

Place your tool shed in the garden, on a porch post or bench or on an outdoor table. Display it where you'll be able to enjoy the fruits of your labor, as well as be able to grab tools for more work.

tool caddy

right: **A quaint toolhouse puts hand tools within reach for quick maintenance tasks. Gloves, trowels, plant markers, and other small helpers wait within.**

tool toting

Keeping tools handy is the key to efficiency in the garden. Options for corralling tools abound. If a cloth garden tote appeals to you, look for washable fabric, plenty of pockets, and a waterproof bottom. Baskets work great, but the tools easily become jumbled; be vigilant about removing unused tools. A 5-gallon bucket with a handle makes a nifty caddy. Pop a lid on it and the bucket becomes a seat for when you weed or take a breather in the garden.

set the stage

above: The best gardens include workhorse features, such as a classic arbor and sturdy chairs, which combine form and function with decorative style. The tool house also fits that bill in this garden. Imagine this scene without the structures.

fountains: bubbling urn

cost	make it	skill
$$$	weekend	moderate

you will need

- container (concrete pot, urn, etc.)
- small submersible pump
- PVC pipe
- silicone sealant
- metal grate or mesh
- reservoir
- flexible 2-layer PVC pond liner
- bricks or flat stones
- plastic electrical conduit
- ground fault interrupter GFCI outlet
- assorted river rocks or cobblestones

backyard bubbler

A fountain brings multiple rewards to any garden. It requires minimal space and adds sound and movement. Trickling water helps mask nearby traffic noise and attracts birds, which bring color and ear-pleasing birdsong to the scene. Involve the whole family in the project and you will create a beautiful water feature for all to enjoy.

where to begin

First, select a vessel for your fountain. Find a one-of-a-kind container at an estate sale, a country auction, or in your own garage. Consider concrete, ceramic, fiberglass, or plastic pots at a local garden center. You'll need to apply concrete sealer to the concrete pot. When purchasing the container, ask if it is watertight.

think bigger
right: Instead of settling for a basic fountain spray head, add a stately urn to your pond's aeration plan.

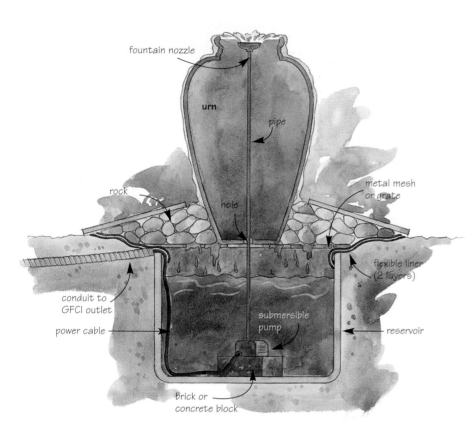

fountain nozzle

urn

pipe

rock

hole

metal mesh
or grate

conduit to
GFCI outlet

power cable

flexible liner
(2 layers)

submersible
pump

reservoir

brick or
concrete block

simple setup

The fountain sits above a reservoir of water. This water can be a pond (*opposite*) or an underground, rock-covered pool (*below left* and in the drawing, *left*). Build a reservoir large enough to capture all the water held in your urn (or similar container) and then some, as it bubbles over into the reservoir. Make the reservoir wider than the urn. A plastic tub works well. Spread two layers of flexible pond liner beneath the surrounding rocks and into the basin to help contain splashing water. Set the submersible pump on a brick or concrete block in the reservoir. Place the metal grate over the reservoir, making sure it's level.

power and water

Ensure that the hole in the bottom of your container accommodates the water delivery pipe from the pump. Use a masonry bit on a power drill to enlarge the hole if necessary. Run the pipe through the hole; seal it with marine silicone.

Install a weatherproof power outlet at least 4 feet away from the fountain. Install a ground fault interrupter outlet (GFCI) in an existing outdoor outlet; or have a GFCI outlet installed by an electrician to prevent shorts and outages in your household circuitry. Run electrical wiring from the GFCI outlet through a conduit and a trench excavated beneath the flexible liner. Connect the power cord from the submersible pump to the wiring or to the outlet.

Set the container in place with the water delivery pipe attached to the pump. Test the pump before proceeding. Make adjustments in the spout height to control the fountain's water jet. When the fountain is running, the top of the pipe should be just below water level. Add stones to cover the metal grate. Run the fountain continually or whenever you desire. Check the water level frequently, adding water as needed.

bargain fountain
left: **A garage-sale find, such as this $2 vase, transforms an ugly-duckling urn into a swan of a fountain and provides instant atmosphere with the sound of sheeting water.**

garden decorating | **145**

fountains

water wizardry

The sight and sound of a gurgling fountain affect
the human psyche. Muscles relax, breathing
deepens, and thoughts wander. Fountains foster
a sense of well-being and tranquility.

Soothe yourself with the magic of splashing
water by starting small. Try a prefabricated tabletop
fountain that nestles neatly into a corner of your
deck or patio. If you're handy and adventurous,
tackle building your own bubbling fountain.
Easily adapt the project on pages 144 and 145
to construct a fountain in a container without
a reservoir. Alternatively, search locally for artists
who craft fountains from hand-cast concrete
poured on forms of wire armature, such as the
columns shown *opposite.*

A fountain acts as a focal point and enhances
a setting. Make fountains part of existing or
planned seating areas. Use them as the anchor
for a new garden area. Or place them near
bedroom windows, where the trickling water
plays a nightly lullaby.

While laying electrical lines for your fountain,
wire the area for night lighting too. Fountains
become almost mystical when lit from underwater
at night using submersible halogen light fixtures.
If working with electricity makes you nervous,
hire an electrician. Keep costs down by digging
the trenching and purchasing the project supplies.

pond trios

right: **This small but alluring pond combines
a fountain and a stone bridge with a nearby
tubful of water lilies to create a supreme
aquatic scene.**

bold boulder
above left: Plumb
a granite rock for
a watery show. Find a
choice specimen at a
quarry. Hire water
garden specialists to
do the rest.

gentle shower
above: Recycle
a bathtub into a
fountain—complete
with a mossy duck!

trickling columns
left: A group of piped
concrete pedestal
fountains, topped
with urns of moisture-
loving plants,
makes an unusual
vertical feature.

fire

fired up

Crackling flames, twinkling stars, and the wonderfully soothing scent of wood smoke provide the threads that weave unforgettable memories. Make your home the destination of choice for family and friends with a fire pit or outdoor fireplace.

Situate any fireplace well away from structures, tree canopies, and neighbors who might be troubled by smoke. Surround it with smooth fireproof surfaces to eliminate tripping hazards. Line the fire pit with firebrick, which withstands high heat. Include a drain (so water doesn't accumulate) and a lid that's flush with the ground (to cover the pit when not in use). Before you break ground, check local building ordinances. If you can't burn leaves in your area, you can't build a backyard fire legally, no matter how well-contained it is.

freestanding fireplace

below: **A common sight in desert gardens, the terra-cotta chiminea has roots in Mexico as a compact patio-warming fireplace ideal for limited spaces.**

Once you've cooked over open flames, you'll never want to go back to traditional grilling. Plan your fire pit with cooking in mind. Find commercially available barbecue hardware that fits the fire pit. Consider adding a grill rack, stainless-steel rotisserie, or whatever gadgets your grilling gourmet likes to use. Custom-built equipment is available, but pricey, through local machinists.

A raised stone wall offers simple but effective seating around a fire pit. If you prefer to use more comfortable seating, such as chairs with backs and cushions, set them far enough from the fire to minimize dangers from heat or sparks.

If you have trouble visualizing a new garden use the online interactive garden-design tool at **www.bhg.com/bkplanagarden**

beauty

enhance
the pleasure

Personal touches transform a house into a home. In the garden, the same effect occurs when gardeners accessorize their outdoor spaces with decor that helps unwind the mind, soothe the soul, and delight the eye. Some of the most creative garden embellishments capitalize on natural resources—wind, water, and light—or found objects to enhance the beauty of life in the garden.

celebrate style Transforming your garden from a grow-place into a showplace need not involve a bundle of money or a professional designer. Let your personality shine through your selection of decorative accents and then watch your garden transform into a homey place.

treasure trove While beauty may be difficult to put into words, you know it when you see it. You experience the lasting pleasures of beauty in the garden: in the splendors of nature, peaceful moments, amazement, inspiration, and various sensual delights.

Whether you're an ardent gardener or more of a garden decorator, you will probably agree that flowers epitomize garden beauty. Of course, tastes vary in terms of perceiving beauty in objets d'art. But the best garden treasures glow with personality, whether gathered in a collection of vintage garden tools or set apart in a handcrafted fountain.

Choose artful elements that provide pleasure at a glance or a touch, or delight merely with their sound. Splash a favorite color around your garden—on fences, cushions, and containers. Color ties together an eclectic setting, tastefully and artistically.

details, details Focus on sensory appeal, and you won't overlook any opportunity to tuck a bit of beauty into your garden. Trickling water or tinkling wind chimes play melodies that will tickle your ears and mask neighborhood noise. Wind art that spins, dances, and bobs in the breeze pleases the eyes, and the more comical ones may even incite a few giggles. Make an enchanted evening in your garden with lanterns, candleholders, and other night lighting.

art: papier-mâché sculpture

cost	make it	skill
$	weekend	easy

you will need

- balloon or chicken wire
- masking tape
- shredded newspaper, junk mail
- powdered cellulose or papier-mâché paste
- blender or food processor
- linseed oil

paper art

Elevate recycling to an art form by turning your piles of junk mail and old newspapers into garden sculpture with a stone look. Papier-mâché provides an easy, inexpensive way to add your handiwork to the garden.

Start by choosing a design and building an armature, or a framework, for your sculpture. Use a balloon as the armature for a head, a sun, or any spherical shape. For other shapes, such as angels, animals, or obelisks, mold chicken wire into a representative shape. Tape sheets of paper over the framework to form a smooth surface.

Shred junk mail and newspaper; place the paper in a tub of water (an old plastic dishpan works well). Soak the paper until it is saturated; then pour off the water. Mix approximately 1 quart of moist paper and 1 ounce of powdered cellulose, or papier-mâché paste (from an art supply store), in a blender or food processor. Adjust the proportions of cellulose and moist paper until you have a thick paste (resembling the consistency of oatmeal); a bit more water may be needed to achieve a workable consistency.

Mold the mixture onto your armature. Sculpt contours on the piece and allow the papier-mâché to dry; then add layers to build dimension. Once the sculpture is complete and dry, waterproof it by brushing on linseed oil. Reapply linseed oil annually to extend the life of your art.

guardian angels
left: Angelic creations, made from junk mail and flour paste, keep watch over the garden. Balanced on cocktail stirrers, wire, and other found objects, these winged wonders are painted with plastic paint commonly used by electricians, which makes them waterproof.

unforgettable face
left: This lifesize sculptural beauty—constructed from recycled paper and cellulose paste—withstands weather with a waterproof seal. Inspiration for three-dimensional designs abounds in books about classical architecture, cultural art forms, and ancient civilizations.

garden decorating | **155**

art: garden-hose fountain

cost	make it	skill
$$	weekend	easy

you will need

- spare garden hoses
- metal plant stand
- metal wash tub
- small submersible pump

what a drip

You'll want to leave the water running in this garden hose when you wind it into an unusual fountain. Tangling lengths of seen-better-days hoses of various colors into a snakey sphere that leaks and drips will be satisfying and pleasing. Materials for your fountain can be found around the house, in the garage, or at a garage sale, flea market, or estate auction.

A metal plant stand makes a sturdy fountain base. Plastic-coated steel or vintage iron frames work well. Place the stand in a basin, metal wash tub, a large ceramic pot, or a galvanized livestock watering tank.

Anchor the stand using bricks, concrete blocks, or sandbags wedged around the legs. Intertwine drained hoses around the plant stand, wrapping until a globe is formed. Extend one hose end out the top of the sphere (water will trickle from here). Extend the other hose end out the bottom, attaching it to a submersible pump set in the water basin. Install a ground fault interrupter outlet on the electrical line that runs to the pump. Add water, turn on the power, and let your pleasure begin.

plumb a fountain

right: **A leaky old garden hose is transformed into a delightfully unique fountain.**

vine balls

organic orbs

Harvest grapevines to make spherical sculptures that look good wherever you drop or dangle them in the garden. Fresh–cut vines have supple stems that wind easily. Harvested and dried vines, however, need softening; soak them in water for several hours. Once the stems can be bent without snapping, the vines will have absorbed enough water. Cut vines in fall, wrap them into loose circlets, and leave them outdoors until taking up this project on a wintry day. Begin by wrapping vines in a circle the size desired. Loop another circle, forming an opposite axis, and secure the intersecting vines with twists of wire. Continue winding vines until you make a sphere of the desired size and density.

round and round

above: Garden orbs, made from crisscrossed and wrapped grapevines, add an unusual textural element to the garden. Display vineballs throughout the garden, placed on flat surfaces or dangled from branches. In winter, string them with white lights for a magical effect.

art: garden characters

a motley crew

Populate your garden with a crew of folk art
creatures, from scarecrows and mannequins to
wildlife replicas. Use them to inject a little humor
into the growing scene. But don't depend on
fanciful topiaries or cleverly outfitted statues to
guard your crops from pillaging birds. Replicas
of people can keep wildlife on the wary side, but
eventually animals figure out that the lady standing
by the garden gate never moves. To shoo pesky
critters that feast on the fruits of your labor, try
this trio of scarecrow–building tricks:

movement Give your scarecrow moving
elements. Cloth streamers or mylar ties, that flutter
in the wind and startle animals that wander near
your garden patch or scratch within the plantings.

light Flickering light agitates birds and discourages
them from landing among your plantings. Give
scarecrows hair made from reflective mylar tape;
string aluminum pie tins or pocket mirrors from
their hands to keep animals on the move.

sound Anything that rattles with the wind will
scare animals, such as aluminum pie tins stuffed
with dry beans, cast–off maracas, a string of hard
plastic objects, or a fluttering pinwheel.

scared silly

right: **A fence post becomes a folksy scarecrow
with the addition of wooden-pole arms and
an inverted sap-bucket head. Black fabric
streamers keep birds wary. An Indian-corn
necklace adds a natural touch.**

potshard princess

left: **Folk-art people with larger-than-life dimensions score big as garden focal points. This beauty, bedecked in white lights and clothed in potshards, braces her arms into a tray that can hold either plants or birdseed.**

pretend pond

below: **Topiary herons, turtle, and frog guard a make-believe water garden. Blue stones substitute for water in this whimsical pond.**

collections

garden gatherings

Collections turn passion into personal style. A hankering for hand tools or painted pots becomes a handsome garden display when artfully arranged en masse. Added to the garden as a group, small items have a big impact that reflects your personality.

To curate a collection, track down garden treasures at estate or house sales or at garden shops. Once you've chosen the object of your desire (such as folk art, star-shape items, or bunnies of any sort), keep an eye out when you travel and tell your friends what you're collecting.

Hunting for collectibles should be part of the fun, so think twice before setting your sights on obscure or pricey antique pieces, such as green-handled tools or handwoven wattle fences, which may be frustratingly hard to find.

inside out

above: Architectural features, such as finials, make a great collection. Part of the beauty of a painted wood piece is the way it cracks and peels with time. Protect wooden treasures by displaying them beneath an eave or on a porch.

roosting wall

right: A wall that beckons like a blank canvas is dressed up with a flock of vintage birdcages and birdhouses.

clay on display

left: Terra-cotta plaques, pots, and sculptures emanate desert style with their earthen tones. Display Mexican terra-cotta away from the elements; it deteriorates when exposed to weather.

used but useful

below: Start a collection with a gathering of functional items, such as galvanized watering cans and vintage pots. Display them on an accessible-but-artful fence shelf.

collective effort

Decorative items with collectible potential abound, depending on what strikes your fancy. Select objects that can withstand weather. Consider these possibilities:

- architectural salvage
- metal garden furniture
- old signs
- pickets
- weather vanes
- vintage metal riding toys

wind: chime

cost	make it	skill
$	2 hours	easy

you will need

- discarded silver cutlery, including one fork
- small sledgehammer
- anvil, wooden block, or similar surface
- vise-grip pliers
- needle-nose pliers
- drill
- heavy fishing line

a true tuning fork

Take cutlery to the trees by making a wind chime. Pure silver plays the prettiest tune; gather it at thrift stores and secondhand shops. Collect spoons, knives, or forks; each piece plays a different tone. For instance, soup spoons sound baritone, while forks trill lighter notes. Flattened pieces play the loveliest melodies. Pound each piece with a small sledgehammer on a hard surface such as a solid wood block or an anvil to flatten it. Drill a hole in the top end of each piece of silverware. For the chime support, bend the outer tines of a fork, as shown (*right*), curling each end into a tiny loop. Use fishing line to attach each of the dangling pieces to the fork loops.

silverware songs

right: **Let the wind play chimes with cast-off cutlery. Mix silverware for a merry melody. Hang the creation where it will be enjoyed most.**

weather vanes

ride the wind

Before high-tech radar and 24-hour weather channels, people kept track of weather with clues from nature. Today, meteorologists track the weather for most folks, using sophisticated equipment, giving their best predictions about what nature has in store.

Glean your own weather wisdom from something as simple as the wind. Install a few wind-driven devices, and begin your own prognostications. Or watch for more subtle clues. For instance, according to weatherlore and science, when the wind incites leaves to turn and show their backs, rain is on the way. If rain comes first and wind second, it will be a severe storm, so pack up your gear and head inside. If you spot yellow skies at sunset, a still day will follow. If you see halos around the sun or moon, it means rain or snow will come soon (the halo is formed by ice crystals in the air).

weather art

above left: A windmill adds motion to the garden and informs of weather changes. Traditional farm elements, such as towering windmills and weather vanes, bring vintage character to gardens.

gusty clues

left: Add a weather vane to your garden and watch what the wind direction reveals about incoming weather (see if your weather predictions improve).

wind

art in motion

Harness the breeze to decorate your garden with delightful motion and sound. The parts and pieces of three-dimensional wind art come to life, singing and dancing in the garden. Puffs of wind transform sometimes still sculptures into dynamic mobiles.

The only difficulty in adding wind-propelled embellishments to the garden comes in whether to choose a whirligig, wind sock, wind chime, or other feature. Choose sculptures to suit your garden's style and size, as well as your budget. Look for solidly constructed features. Copper, glass, brass, acrylic, mylar laminate, and wooden pieces are usually durable. A weatherproofed piece is best.

on the wing

right: **As a counterweighted sculpture, this hummingbird balances atop a sturdy metal pole, bobbing, swiveling, and adding playful motion to the garden.**

spin art

below: **Brass and copper marry in a metal sculpture that swings with a puff of wind. The most dynamic wind-driven rigs feature many movable parts, like this coiled and cupped windcatcher.**

volcanic music

left: **Obsidian, a dark glass formed from molten lava, plays a tinkling tune when strummed by a breeze. To prevent damage, hang glass chimes in a protected location.**

wind propellers

below: **Turn your woodworking talents loose to create a whirligig that's intriguing and colorful. Paint wind-driven items in hues to match your garden's palette.**

Select a sculpture that offers a distinct movement, such as whirling, spinning, swiveling, or rocking. Secure your wind art with mounting hardware (if provided with the piece), a metal stake, or a nylon string.

music in the air

Wind chimes take a garden into another dimension. When choosing chimes, consider their sound and appearance. Select traditional metal tube chimes to play exquisitely harmonized chords. For a more exotic look and sound, hang bamboo pipes that resonate with mellow notes or seashells that chatter in the breeze. Glass sings a melodic song; ceramic and polished stones resound with pleasant pitches.

Hang wind chimes in a high, exposed spot, such as under house eaves, for the most constant music. Locate chimes in a somewhat protected spot and shorten the hanger to diminish their sound, or place them strategically in your garden to keep you alerted to the weather. Hang wind chimes outdoors year-round, but be considerate of your neighbor's hearing when you place your chimes.

On the softer side, consider a flag, windsock, or windspinner that flutters or whirls in rippling color. Typically made from plastic or cloth, those with permanently dyed, military-grade polyester or nylon threads resist heat and light for the longest wear and least tear. Dangle banners and flags from a pole that includes an antitangling wrap; or hang them from the eave of an outbuilding. Preserve your fabric art by storing it indoors over winter if you live in a region with a harsh climate.

water

wet and wonderful

Water represents such an integral part of gardening that its possibilities might be overlooked. Water enhances garden decor with pleasing attributes, including sound, light reflection, and motion.

Still water in a reflective pool adds allure to any garden setting. Its depth mirrors the sky and provides mysterious appeal. With plants or not, a quiet pool creates a cool, soothing atmosphere. Make the most of the water's calming effect by placing seating nearby. Poke garden torches in nearby soil or float candles on the water's surface to multiply the flames' reflective dance.

Work water into your garden's decorating scheme by adding a containerized feature or a pond, a stream, or a waterfall. The sound of moving water, whether it splashes, trickles, or bubbles, promotes a sense of tranquility.

Create a simple recirculating fountain in a watertight container. In a small garden, use a jar or bowl fountain that overflows into a below-ground basin, or an elegant wall fountain that spouts into a container below it. A traditional tiered fountain or spouting statuary suits a large or formal garden.

A low, jet-type fountain splashing over pebbles and into an underground reservoir suits almost any garden and attracts wildlife, such as birds and dragonflies. It provides a safe water feature for a garden where children play. An added bonus is the rainbows that form when sunlight strikes the airborne water droplets. Ordinarily, however, you'll

wacky water

right: **Here's a leaky faucet you won't want repaired. The secret of this recirculating fountain is a small submersible pump inside the watering can that pumps water to a pipe running through a hole drilled near the base of the can and attached to a spigot. A screen placed over the hole inside the can catches debris.**

want to locate your water feature in a partly shady place to prevent evaporation and slow the breeding of bacteria.

The sound of a fountain can drown out traffic noise. However, strive for balance. Avoid creating a water feature that sounds like Niagara Falls.

If you're concerned that a constant water supply will attract proliferating mosquitoes, take a preventive tack. Add a couple of goldfish to a pond, pool, or containerized feature; they eat mosquito larvae. Or float a mosquito control ring (available commercially) on the water. It kills mosquito larvae as it dissolves over the weeks but won't harm fish, plants, or people.

garden reflections
above left: A water mirror reflects plants and sky. Choose an elegant container, paint the interior midnight blue, and fill it to the brim.

rain-chain tunes
left: A resin-sealed bamboo gutter catches rain that strums the chain in watery tones.

garden decorating | **167**

water

water pots

If you want to install a water garden yourself and have not dealt with plumbing or electrical projects before, try making a simple trickling fountain using pre-made containers, such as decorative pots that match your graden's style, to boost your confidence before you tackle larger-scale water features.

Nothing is more pleasant than the sight and sound of water flowing through your garden. Find out how to create beautiful water gardens at **www.bhg.com/ bkwatergardens**

terra-cotta trickle

right: **This streaming fountain celebrates the beauty of classic water jars. Because this fountain cannot sustain freezing temperatures, the water must be drained and the jars stored indoors before cold weather arrives.**

artfully colored

left: A small, contained fountain nestles into a corner of the patio and splashes throughout the summer. Silvery lamb's-ears contrasts with the blue tones of the Japanese pot and flat-bottomed bowl.

water on the move

below left: A copper sculpture comes to life, swirling, spraying, and creating kinetic water art when attached to a garden hose. Look for sprinkler designs that feature copper fixtures, several spinning parts, and even reflective glass baubles.

asian touch

below: Pair a bamboo pipe with a stone bowl to make water music in your garden. Adjust the trickling water to a pace that's pleasing; fill the basin with pebbles to modify the sound.

garden decorating | **169**

lighting: paper lanterns

cost	make it	skill
$	3 hours	easy

you will need

- 2 lampshades with socket rings (per lantern)
- bolt cutter
- fabric seam binding
- corrugated paper
- scissors
- twine
- crafts glue
- metal clips
- twine
- colored paper
- votive candle holder
- votive candle

outdoor lighting

Decorate your garden with more than daytime enjoyment in mind. Handmade paper lanterns lit with votive candles cast a soft glow that's perfect for evenings among the flowers.

Gardeners rarely walk through their patches of tended earth during the day without stopping to pull a weed, straighten a stake, or tug off a dead bloom. It's not that the dirty-knees crowd is a compulsive bunch; it's that the garden is an ever-changing place, and the to-do list grows as quickly as the plants. It takes more than planting some cozy-cushioned seats in a strategic part of the garden to guarantee you'll stop to smell your roses. Night lighting offers an irresistible option. In the dim light, even the most obsessive gardener can't see weeds to pull them. Keep the lights low, and you'll discover the wonders of night in your garden. Allow yourself to sit back and savor the flowers' fragrance and the insects' evening songs.

candlelight and flowers
right: **Complement your glowing lanterns with a fragrant evening garden of moonflower, vining petunia, flowering tobacco, evening primrose, datura, and heliotrope.**

1 cut For each lantern, start with two lampshade frames (six-paneled or similar) equipped with socket rings. Remove the ring from one of the frames using bolt cutters. This frame forms the top of the lantern. Remove any material covering the shades leaving bare frames. Place the frames' bottoms together and wrap with seam binding; secure the fabric by tying the ends. Make a lantern-panel template of cardboard and use it to cut medium-weight corrugated paper (from an art supply store).

2 glue Before gluing, tie three lengths of twine to the top of the frame (where you removed the ring socket) spaced evenly apart. Tie the other three ends together in a knot. Use crafts glue to attach the paper panels to the top lampshade frame. Hold panels in place with metal clips until glue dries. Flip the lantern over and glue the panels in place on the second lampshade frame. Glue strips of colored paper in place to cover all the seams.

3 hang Set a votive candleholder in the socket ring; add candle. Hang lanterns from tree branches, a pergola, or an arbor using S-shape hooks. Trim excess twine to keep it safely away from candle flames. To reduce fire hazard, avoid using lanterns on windy evenings. Paper lanterns should not hang outdoors overnight. One night's dew can warp the paper. Decorate your lanterns with decoupage, pressed dried leaves, or pressed dried flowers pasted to the insides of the panels before gluing them onto the frame.

garden decorating | **171**

lighting: sea-glass lantern

cost	make it	skill
$	½ hour	easy

you will need

votive candle
or tealight

two clear glass
cylindrical vases
(one wider than
the other)

sea glass

just beachy

Add a little nightlife to your garden with an easy handcrafted candle that's elegant enough for the most formal indoor setting. The gentle light of a candle becomes a shimmering glow as it shines through a layer of frosty sea glass (pieces tossed, sculpted, and worn by waves).

To add candles to your garden that won't go out as the evening breezes stir, tuck them into deep containers that protect them from wind. Start with two cylindrical glass vases in graduated sizes, available from florist suppliers and crafts stores. Slip a votive candle inside the smaller cylinder, and place that inside the larger vase. Fill the spaces between the two cylinders with clear or colored sea glass, also available from crafts stores.

glassy glow

When the sun sets and the crickets begin to chirp, a handful of candles and a string of twinkle lights unlock the mystery of the evening garden. The real beauty of twilight garden illuminations emerges as a small investment yields large results in light, charm, and unforgettable ambience.

carrying a torch

right and *opposite top:* The secret to keeping flames tamed to a gentle flicker in the garden is to protect them from the winds. Tuck candles into deep glass cups to shelter the flames.

more night lights

Float candles in a deep birdbath, or tuck votives or tea lights inside clear, colored, or frosted glass cups, lanterns, or lamps. Drape electric lights over shrubs, and wrap strings of lights around tree branches overhanging seating areas. Oil lamps burn the longest and strongest, providing a clear, steady flame for hours on end. Take care to wipe up any oil spills with a clean rag; carefully dispose of the rag to avoid a fire hazard.

chimney-cap lanterns

Turn inexpensive, galvanized chimney covers (available at hardware stores) into sleek, unusual lanterns. Spray paint the chimney covers with exterior-grade enamel; let dry. Drill holes along the edge of the chimney cap from which to dangle rocks. Wrap thin wire around smooth river stones and feed a wire through each hole; snip off any excess wire after you have wrapped and hung each stone. Center the chimney cap over a votive candle. The chimney cover will become extremely hot as the candle burns. Use heat-resistant mitts, or allow caps to cool completely before handling them. Avoid placing lanterns where children, guests, or pets might come in contact with them.

lighting: wooden lanterns

cost	make it	skill
$$–$$$	weekend	moderate

you will need

- low-voltage light set
- four cedar fence panels (see dimensions on plan, *opposite*)
- pencil compass
- power drill
- jigsaw
- table saw
- exterior wood glue
- 4d finishing nails
- #6 ¾-inch brass roundhead wood screws
- carpenter's square
- nail set
- sandpaper
- exterior varnish
- wood putty

night lights

Low-voltage outdoor lights are easy to install and add ambience, safety, and security to your landscape. But the garden-variety plastic fixtures could do with a makeover in wood.

Choose from four handsome wood-surround designs to dress up a light set (available from retail and mail-order sources) to suit your garden's style. Build the surrounds of weather-resistant wood such as cedar, redwood, or cypress. The plans (*opposite*) use standard cedar-fencing panels to construct covers that beautify the ordinary lights, transforming them into a decorative asset. If you don't feel up to the task of building the surrounds, hire a carpenter to make them for you. The low-voltage light set you purchase will determine the number of surrounds you'll need.

When installing the lanterns, bury the bottom 2 or 3 inches of the surrounds for stability, or secure them to a wooden stake hidden inside or on the backside of each surround.

lighting quartet
above: Choose from four lamp designs to make your softly glowing lanterns, featuring *(clockwise)* a plain pedestal style, a beveled cover, a chamfered cover, or a copper top.

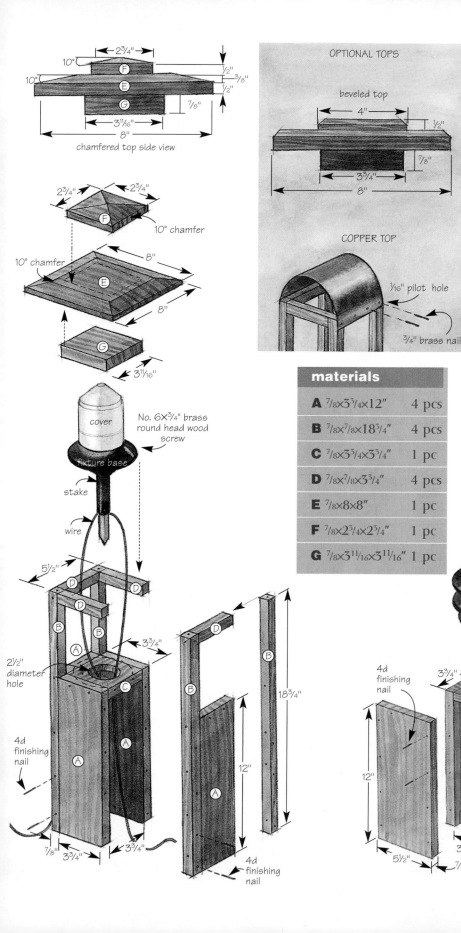

chamfered top side view

2¾"
10°
10°
½"
³⁄₈"
½"
⁷⁄₈"
3¹¹⁄₁₆"
8"

2¾"
2¾"
10° chamfer
10° chamfer
8"
8"
3¹¹⁄₁₆"

cover

No. 6×¾" brass round head wood screw

fixture base

stake

wire

5½"

2½" diameter hole

3¾"

4d finishing nail

18¾"

12"

12"

⁷⁄₈"
3¾"
3¾"
4d finishing nail

5½"
⁷⁄₈"
3¾"
3¾"

OPTIONAL TOPS

beveled top

4"
½"
⁷⁄₈"
3¾"
8"

COPPER TOP

¹⁄₁₆" pilot hole

¾" brass nail

materials

A ⁷⁄₈×3¾×12"	4 pcs
B ⁷⁄₈×⁷⁄₈×18¾"	4 pcs
C ⁷⁄₈×3¾×3¾"	1 pc
D ⁷⁄₈×⁷⁄₈×3¾"	4 pcs
E ⁷⁄₈×8×8"	1 pc
F ⁷⁄₈×2¾×2¾"	1 pc
G ⁷⁄₈×3¹¹⁄₁₆×3¹¹⁄₁₆"	1 pc

2½" diameter hole

4d finishing nail

3¾"

lovely lanterns

The lanterns (*opposite*) were built using ⁷⁄₈-inch-thick cedar fencing, which is smooth on one side and rough on the other. If you use a different thickness of wood, adjust the dimensions to make each surround 5½-inches square. Cut all the wood pieces to size. Mark a 2½-inch-diameter hole centered on each lamp support (C) to fit the plastic fixture base. Cut the hole with a jigsaw.

To build the chamfer-style unit shown at *far left*, first connect the wiring and lights, following instructions in your light set. Slide a stake and fixture through the hole in part C. Attach the fixture base to the lamp support using two brass screws (predrill holes through each fixture base). Add the plastic cover to the light base.

Then construct the covered surrounds, by gluing and nailing one side (A) and one rail (D) between two uprights (B), keeping the surfaces and the ends flush. Repeat to create a second panel, then nail and glue these two preassembled panels to the lamp support. Glue and nail the remaining two sides (A) and two rails (D) between the existing panels to complete the surround. Check the corners for a 90-degree angle. Use a nail set to countersink nails slightly.

Build the tops last; Cut chamfered tops using a table saw.

Sand the surrounds and their tops until smooth. Allow them to weather naturally or apply an exterior finish such as spar varnish. If you use a finish, apply one coat and allow it to dry. Fill in the nail holes using wood putty matching the wood finish. Apply a second coat of finish.

lighting: blue glass votives

cost	make it	skill
$	2 hours	easy

you will need

- glass jars or vases
- spray paint
- plastic saucer
- votive candles

sky blue

Pint-size canning jars, glazed with paint to match a garden's decorating scheme, provide pretty and low-cost candle lanterns. The blue-hued jars enhance the garden scene while protecting the candles from breezes.

A garden that gets the blues can be a pretty thing. Just coordinate all the accessories in your garden as shown with an easy-to-apply coat of paint or matching ready-made items. A single-color theme ties together incongruous pieces, from mismatched furniture to odd pots and other elements. Choose decorative fabrics and tableware featuring the same color.

Surround your color-drenched setting with flowers that bloom in complementary hues. In this case, yellow, orange, pink, and white make excellent plant companions for the blue scheme. If you're unsure what color to use, browse paint chips at your local home improvement or paint store.

hot stuff

right and *far right:* Use long matches to light short candles tucked inside jars. Or use a handheld propane lighter with a long nozzle (often sold alongside grilling products).

1 gather jars Select the containers you want as candleholders. Glass jars of any kind, vases, or deep bowls work well. Match candles to containers. Wide-mouth containers up to 6 inches tall can hold small pillar candles. Tea lights fit easily inside half-pint glass jars or shallow bowls. Use a wide, shallow disposable container, such as a plastic pot saucer, when glazing the glass containers.

2 prepare the palette Glaze your glassware with an acetone-base spray paint because it will float on the water's surface. Use a floral-type spray paint (Design Master No. 743, deep blue, *shown*), formulated for spraying color on fresh or dried flowers and available from a crafts store or floral supplier. Fill the plastic saucer with water. Spray a light coat of paint on the water's surface.

3 dip and swirl Create the soft mottled effect on the glass by dipping each container into the water and rotating it once to glaze it with paint. Coating the glass with too much paint diminishes the glazed effect. Do not use this method for tableware used for serving or eating. The paint won't hold up to repeated washings. To paint statuary with a similar effect, mist statues with water before spraying on paint.

lighting

night lights

Outdoor lighting woven through your garden adds warmth, magic, and glow. Use candles, string lights, torches, or lanterns. Amplify the brightening effect by siting reflective surfaces nearby, such as water or a gazing ball. White flowers and light-colored surfaces also gleam with a subtle luminescence when accompanied by light.

Candles offer a simple but spellbinding touch. Before including candles in your garden, however, follow these basic safety tips:

- Keep a bucket of water, a garden hose, or a fire extinguisher nearby.
- Before handling metal or glass candle accessories, allow them to cool or wear heat-resistant barbecue mitts.
- Trim candle wicks to ¼ inch before lighting.
- Place unenclosed candles away from leaves and flammable fabrics.
- Fit candles snugly in their holders.
- Store matches and lighters in a secure place away from open flames and children.
- When not in use, store candles indoors or turn their containers over to prevent rain and dirt from accumulating.
- To remove melted wax from containers, store them in the freezer for two hours before gently prying off the wax. To remove soot, fill the container with hot sudsy water; allow the container to soak for several hours before scrubbing it.
- Keep all lit candles out of reach from children and pets.

floral flotilla

right: **Terra-cotta saucers filled with water, choice blooms, leaves, and floating candles make an attractive centerpiece. White candles work well with any color of flowers and foliage; keep plenty on hand for the gardening season.**

dynamic duo
above left: Dragonfly string lights pair handsomely with tea lights.

buzz on
above: Linen bags, stamped with fabric ink and stuffed with plastic wrap make white twinkle lights dazzle.

candles ahoy
left: Stand a twine-tied bouquet in a wide-mouth vase; add rocks, water, and floating candles for spectacular results.

resources

bird supplies

Duncraft
102 Fisherville Rd.
Concord, NH 03303
800/593-5656
www.duncraft.com

book

Making Bentwood Trellises, Arbors, Gates & Fences
Long Creek Herb Farm
P.O. Box 127
Blue Eye, MO 65611
417/779-5450
www.longcreekherbs.com

containers

Classic Garden Ornaments, Ltd.
Longshadow Gardens
83 Longshadow Lane
Pomona, IL 62975
618/893-4831
www.longshadow.com

A Garden of Distinction
5819 Sixth Ave. S.
Seattle, WA 98108
206/763-0517
www.agardenofdistinction.com

copper sprinklers

BirdBrain, Inc.
P.O. Box 130265
Ann Arbor, MI 48113
734.483.4536
www.birdbrain.com

everything gardening (furniture, ornaments, structures, containers, fountains, lighting)

Charleston Gardens
61 Queen Street
Charleston, SC 29401
800/469-0118
www.charlestongardens.com

Frontgate
5566 West Chester Road
West Chester, OH 45069
800/626-6488
www.frontgate.com

Gardeners Eden
17 Riverside St.
Nashua, NH 03062
800/822-9600
www.gardenerseden.com

Garden Pals
3825 Manitou Ct.
Mira Loma, CA 91752
800/666-4044
www.gardenpals.com

Gardener's Supply Co.
128 Intervale Rd.
Burlington, VT 05401
888/833-1412
www.gardeners.com

Kinsman Co. Inc.
P.O. Box 428
Pipersville, PA 18947
800/733-4146
www.kinsmangarden.com

Smith & Hawken
P.O. Box 431
Milwaukee, WI 53201-0431
800/940-1170
www.smithandhawken.com

fountains & supplies

Hughes Water Gardens
25289 S.W. Stafford Rd.
Tualatin, OR 97062
503/638-1709; 800/858-1709
www.watergardens.com

Springdale Water Gardens
340 Old Quarry Lane
P.O. Box 546
Greenville, VA 24440-0546
800/420-5459
www.springdalewatergardens.com

Stone Forest
P.O. Box 2840
Santa Fe NM, 87504
888/682-2987
www.stoneforest.com

garden art

Garden Artisans
Rt. 1, Box 1079-Q5,
Townsend, GA 31331
912/437-2270
www.gardenartisans.com

George Carruth
221 Mechanic St.
Waterville, OH 43566
419/878-5412
www.carruthstudio.com

garden structures

Arboria
LWO Corp.
P.O. Box 17125
Portland, OR 97217
503/286-5372
www.arboria.com

Bloomsbury Market
403 S. Cedar Lake Road
Bryn Mawr, MN 55405
800/999-2411
www.bloomsburymkt.com

Trellis Structures
60 River St.
Beverly, MA 01915
888/285-4624
www.trellisstructures.com

Walpole Woodworkers
767 East St., Route 27
Walpole, MA 02081
800/343-6948
www.walpolewoodworkers.com

greenhouses
Santa Barbara Greenhouses
721 Richmond Ave.
Oxnard CA 93030
800/544-5276
www.sbgreenhouse.com

Sundance Supply
P.O. Box 225
Olga, WA 98279
800/776-2534
www.sundancesupply.com

hammocks
Nags Head Hammocks
Milepost 9 Highway 158
Nags Head, NC 27959
800/344-6433
www.nagshead.com

lighting
Buy-Solar.com
73 Glenwood Ave.
Demarest, NJ 07527
800/837-6527

Intermatic Inc.
Intermatic Plaza
Spring Grove, IL 60081-9698
800/492-2289

Stone Manor Lighting
9612 Porterdale Rd.
Malibu, CA 90265
888/534-0544
www.stonemanorlighting.com

firepits & patio fireplaces
Exterior Accents
9931-B Rose Commons Drive
Huntersville, NC 28078
888/551-5211
www.exterior-accents.com

Final Touches
P.O. Box 2557
115 Morris Street
Blowing Rock, NC 28605
877/506-2741 (toll free)
www.finaltouches.com

Fire Science Inc.
8350 Main Street
Williamsville, NY 14221
716/633-1130
www.fire-science.com

outdoor fabrics & cushions
Outdoor Fabrics
P.O. Box 160466
Miami, FL 33116
800/640-3539
www.outdoorfabrics.com

Sunbrella
Glen Raven Custom Fabrics
1831 N. Park Ave.
Glen Raven, NC 27217-1100
336/221-2211
www.sunbrella.com

wind chimes & wind art
Imagine That! Windchimes
240 Curnutt Lane
Ten Mile, TN 37880
423/334-4629
www.imaginethatchimes.com

Music in the Wind
P.O. Box 812
Silverton, OR 97381
877/946-3687
www.musicinthewind.com

Toland Enterprises
1750 South Lane
Mandeville, LA 70471
888-933-5620
www.tolandnet.com

Wind & Weather
1200 N. Main St.
Fort Bragg, CA 95437
800-922-9463
www.windandweather.com

wooden swings, benches, & gliders
The Cedar Store
1620 Rt. 8
Glenshaw, PA 15116
888/293-2339
www.cedarstore.com

Creative Woodworking
7261 Highway 43 S.
Spruce Pine, AL 35585
888/225-2029
www.oakswings.com

Plow & Hearth
P.O. Box 6000
Madison, VA 22727-1600
800/627-1712
www.plowhearth.com

index

index

index

index

index

photo credit

Chris Jacobson
GARDENART
157 (bottom right)

metric conversions

u.s. units to metric equivalents

to convert from	multiply by	to get
Inches	25.400	Millimeters
Inches	2.540	Centimeters
Feet	30.480	Centimeters
Feet	0.3048	Meters
Yards	0.9144	Meters
Square inches	6.4516	Square centimeters
Square feet	0.0929	Square meters
Square yards	0.8361	Square meters
Acres	0.4047	Hectares
Cubic inches	16.387	Cubic centimeters
Cubic feet	0.0283	Cubic meters
Cubic feet	28.316	Liters
Cubic yards	0.7646	Cubic meters
Cubic yards	764.550	Liters

metric units to u.s. equivalents

to convert from	multiply by	to get
Millimeters	0.0394	Inches
Centimeters	0.3937	Inches
Centimeters	0.0328	Feet
Meters	3.2808	Feet
Meters	1.0936	Yards
Square centimeters	0.1550	Square inches
Square meters	10.764	Square feet
Square meters	1.1960	Square yards
Hectares	2.4711	Acres
Cubic centimeters	0.0610	Cubic inches
Cubic meters	35.315	Cubic feet
Liters	0.0353	Cubic feet
Cubic meters	1.308	Cubic yards
Liters	0.0013	Cubic yards

To convert from degrees Celsius (C) to degrees Fahrenheit (F), multiply by $\frac{9}{5}$, then add 32.

To convert from degrees Fahrenheit (F) to degrees Celsius (C), first subtract 32, then multiply by $\frac{5}{9}$.